Parsi, Jaina and Sikhs

OR

Some Minor Religious Sects in India

Parsi, Jaina and Sikhs

OR

Some Minor Religious Sects in India

Douglas M. Thornton

KALPAZ

ISBN: 978-93-5128-585-4

First Published in 1898
Indian Reprint in 2017

Published by

Kalpaz Publications
C-30, Satyawati Nagar,
Delhi – 110052
E-mail: kalpaz@hotmail.com
Website: kalpazpublications.com
Ph.: +91-9212142040

PREFACE

WITH A WORD OF INTRODUCTION

AMIDST the many evolutions of Indian religious thought, there is often a danger of losing sight of individual influences at work. The selection of these three religious sects of Parsi, Jaina, and Sīkh will, it is hoped, stimulate further study of those ages of religious inquiry which have given birth to so many schools of thought. The Parsi and the Sīkh religions are of twofold interest, as being religious faiths that have given birth to nations.

Parsi-ism has, therefore, been treated more from an historical than a present-day standpoint, which latter fails to give a true impression of its value as a study. The Parsi can rightly claim to have encouraged the study of philology, and of the comparative method of investigating the religions of the world.

The distinctive tenets of the Jaina take us, for their origin, back to the Buddhist era in India—that greatest era of religious speculation that the world has ever known. And hence the study of Jaina philosophy throws many side-lights on the origin of Buddhism and the period which gave it birth. It is time that this were recognized more widely by Anglo-Indians.

The Sīkh remind us of the entrance of Islām into India, and the era of its struggle with reforming Hindūism. Their faith embodies both the pantheism of the Brāhman and the monotheism of the Mūslim, being itself the product of the reflections of successive teachers under both these influences.

D. M. T.

All Saints' Day, 1898.

CONTENTS

CHAPTER I

THE PARSI

CHAPTER II

THE JAINA

CHAPTER III

THE SĪKH

CHAPTER I

THE PARSI

'I form the light, and create darkness; I make peace, and create evil; I am the Lord, that doeth all these things.'—ISA. xlv. 7 (R.V.).

I. Parsi-ism and its place in history—Ancient and modern knowledge of Zoroastrianism — Biblical, classical, mediaeval, European.

II. The Parsi Scriptures—Definition of Avesta, Zand, Pahlavi, Pāzand, and Huzvāriṣ—The language of the Zend-Avesta—Its original extent—The formation of a Canon—Present contents—Methods of interpretation.

III. The origin and founder of Zoroastrianism—The personality of Zoroaster—His age and birthplace—Zoroastrian theology before Alexander—The Magi—Aryan and Iranian elements.

IV. The ritual of the Zend-Avesta—Birth, marriage, and burial ceremonies—The towers of silence.

V. Parsi history—The Mohammedan conquest of Persia—Emigration to India—Present population, mortality, and occupations—Parsi costumes, sects, calendar, festivals, laws, and government.

I.

Parsi-ism and its Place in History.

THE history of the world is full of eras when momentous changes have happened suddenly, as well as of long periods of progress and decay between the storms of action. Migrations of the human race, and rise of kingdoms in the East and West, have caused a series of great shocks when nations meet. And as the monuments of the past unravel history, it is remarkable to see how often boundaries of Western Asia have become this meeting-place; and how the times of meeting mark the promulgation of some new and great religion of the world.

The age of Abraham and period of the Kings are known to be an age of strife between the dynasties of Africa and Asia, while ancient Israel lay between the two. The period of Achaemenian kings and Medo-Persian empire marks the rise of Zoroastrianism. And though the East received its checks at Marathon and Salamis, the brilliant short career of Alexander added to the doctrines of the Magi Western culture, and wider scope of influence on Greek philosophy and Jewish thought; while, on the other side, an open door from India made a way of entrance into Persia for the teachings of the Brāhman and the Buddha. Lastly, the Roman empire and universal peace prepared three continents to receive the Christ of God, until Mohammed's holy war stirred up the lingering forces of disintegration in the East and West.

Ancient and Modern Knowledge of Zoroastrianism.

The history of research into the religion of Zoroaster has been well divided into three periods—the classical, the mediaeval, and the modern inquiries. But only a few important names and authorities will be mentioned here, gathered from Jewish, Greek, Roman, Armenian, Mohammedan, and European sources.

Bible Witness.

The Old Testament contains two allusions to the Magi and their worship; in Jer. xxxix. 3 'Rab Mag,' or 'the chief of the Magi,' figures as an influential member of Nebuchadrezzar's party, proving that they had reached Babylon by 600 B.C.; and in Ezek. viii. 16, where their worship of the sun is hinted at. Besides these passages there is much indirect evidence that Cyrus held beliefs somewhat similar to the Hebrew captives (cf. Isa. xliv. 28, xlv. 1, xlvi. 11). While in the New Testament the 'adoration of the

Magi' at 'the Epiphany of Christ' is of historic interest (Matt. ii. 1).

Classical Witness.

Greek and Latin writers about the Magi are very numerous. Among those who have given the best information are to be found, Herodotus (450 B.C.), Ktesias (400 B.C.), Theopompus (300 B.C.), and Hermippus (250 B.C.). The latter is quoted by both Pliny and Plutarch as having made elaborate investigations (now lost) into all Zoroastrian books. Eudoxus and Aristotle are quoted by Diogenes of Laerte as having grasped the dualistic doctrine of the Magi. Among later writers Strabo (60 B.C.), Dio Chrysostomus (130 A.D.), Pausanias (180 A.D.), Berosus, Damascius, and Theodorus figure, and give respectively histories of the fire-worship, theology, and dualism of the Persians.

Mediaeval Witness.

Two Armenians, Eznik and Elisaeus, denounced their heresies and compiled a history in the fifth century A.D. Then came Masudi, the famous Arab historian and traveller (950 A.D.), with more reliable information on the Avesta, the Zand, and the Pāzand. He dated Zoroaster at 610 B.C., and did much to explain the meaning of words. Two centuries later Shrahrastani wrote 'on Religious Sects and Creeds.' Though a Mohammedan, he gives a most favourable account of the Magi, and classifies them with great discretion among the Jews, Christians, and Mohammedans as having their creed founded on revealed books. He reported several Magian sects as existing at the time (1153 A.D. obit). But during all the time of the Middle Ages the ignorance of Western writers about the Magi was profound.

European Witness.

After the Renaissance inquiries began again. 'And the nations of modern Europe came into contact with the adherents of the Zoroastrian religion in the western part of India, where they had settled, when they left their fatherland, Persia, to escape the persecutions of the Mohammedans.' *Thomas Hyde* (of Oxford) has the honour of making the first deep research into the classics upon the subject. But he knew not the Avesta language. It was *Anquetil Duperron* whose example inspired others to follow. He furnished Europe with 180 MSS. of several Oriental languages for research, and gave a general outline of the contents of the Avesta to the literary world in 1771. He had his critics in Sir William Jones, Richardson, Meniers, and Tychsen, but *Kleuker* proved the authenticity of his work from the classics, and *Rask* proved the close affinity of the Avesta with Sanskrit. As early as 1793 Sylvestre de Sacy began to decipher Sassanian Inscriptions. Then *Eugene Burnouf*, the Frenchman, became the founder of Avesta philology, and published the first edition of Avesta texts which had appeared in Europe (1829–43). He showed the value of Neryosangh's Sanskrit translation of the greater part of the Avesta, but never having studied Pahlavi his work proved incomplete. After him followed a number of German scholars, such as Olshausen, Bopp, and Müller; Friederic Spiegel, Hermann Brockhaus, Westergaard, and Martin Haug; of lesser lights—Duncker, Lassen, Windischmann, Bleeck, and Justi; while more recently West, Mills, De Harlez, and Darmesteter have come to the front.

A longer notice is due to some of these scholars.

Hermann Brockhaus, the Sanskrit Professor at Leipsic, was the first to publish a rudimentary Avesta dictionary (1850), and an edition of the Vandīdād Sāda in Roman characters with index and glossary. This book did much to stimulate Avesta studies in Germany.

Friederic Spiegel aimed at giving the world a critical edition of the whole of the writings in the Avesta language, based upon a comparison of all the MSS.

then extant in Europe, which chiefly lay in Copenhagen, Paris, London, and Oxford. His researches have been of great value. He brought out a grammar of Pāzand (1851), and also of Huzvāriṣ (1856–60), thus unravelling some of the most difficult pieces of work that the philologist had to do. Then came his two volumes of Avesta translation (1853–8).

Westergaard collected his information from all Europe, India, and Persia. He, first, discovered the Gātha to be metrical pieces, and then published Avesta texts (1854). But he was too cautious to translate quickly. His texts are admirable and have never been superseded.

Haug built upon Brockhaus' compilation and Westergaard's Yasna text. Then he tried to study the Gātha, and found Anquetil's translation useless. Foiled in this, he studied the Veda, Armenian, Pahlavi, and modern Persian, to enable him to collect all the parallel passages in the Zend-Avesta and arrange them. He found the Veda the most useful for his purpose, and brought out his work *The Five Gāthas* (1858–60). Appointed as Sanskrit Professor in Poona College, he continued his researches, especially in Gūjarat for MSS. (1863–4). A further study of Pahlavi and Huzvāriṣ somewhat modified his views on the supposed antagonism between Veda and Avesta antecedents. Several works have been published by him (1868–74), while he was Professor at Munich. His famous *Essays on the Parsis* have been edited in England by Mr. E. W. West, and form a standard work upon the subject.

West began to help Haug in his revision of his last work on the Parsi Religion, *The Book of Arḍā-Vīrāf* (1872), and its glossary (1874) of Pahlavi-Pāzand. He has also published several other works, e.g. *The Book of the Mainyō-ī-khard;* but he is specially noted for his *Pahlavi Texts* in the Oxford series of 'Sacred Books of the East' (vols. v, xviii, xxiv, xxxvii), which came out between 1880 and 1892.

Darmesteter proved himself to be a genius in 1875, when he brought out his *Essay on the Mythology of the Avesta.* To him has been entrusted the translation of the Zend-Avesta in the Oxford series. Vols. iv, xxiii are his (vol. xxxi being due to Mr. L. H. Mills, and consisting of the Yasna, Visparad, and parts of the Khord-Avesta). Especially valuable is his introduction to vol. iv (second edition, 1895), which has been largely used in the following pages.

De Harlez brought out a translation of the Avesta (1881), with some useful discussions in the introduction.

II.

The Parsi Scriptures.

The common name given to the Parsi Sacred Books, by Europeans, is the Zend-Avesta. This term has found favour in Europe, since the days of Anquetil Duperron; but it is rather a misleading name. So it will be well to clear the ground at the start, and decide upon what each term means, in order to avoid all ambiguity later on.

There are five words used in connexion with the Parsi Scriptures, and needing some explanation. They are—*Avesta, Zand, Pahlavi, Pāzand,* and *Huzvāriṣ.* Mr. West has put very clearly the proper relationship between the first three of these terms when he says—'The Avesta and Pahlavi of the same scripture, taken together, form its Avesta and Zand, terms which are nearly synonymous with "revelation and commentary." European scholars, misled probably by Mohammedan writers, have converted the phrase "Avesta and Zand" into "Zend-Avesta," and have further identified Zand with the language of the Avesta[1].' Then he proceeds to explain that 'this use of the word Zand is quite at variance with the practice of all Parsi writers who

[1] S. B. E., vol. v., *Pahlavi Texts*, pt. i. p. x.

have been independent of European influences, as they apply the term Zand only to the Pahlavi translations and explanations of their sacred books, the original text of which they call Avesta. So that when they use the phrase "Avesta and Zand," they mean the whole of any scripture, both the Avesta text and Pahlavi translation and commentary[1].'

Haug, however, has a further explanation of how the term Zend-Avesta came to be widely used. He says—'It is probable that the term Zend was originally applied to commentaries written in the same language as the Avesta, for in the Pahlavi translation of the Yasna, when the scriptures are mentioned, both terms, "Avistāk va Zand," are used, as if of equal authority[2]." At any rate the later (or Pahlavi) Zand appears also in many places to be merely a translation of this earlier (or Avesta) Zand, with additional explanations offered by the Pahlavi translators. In this case, Zend-Avesta would not be a wholly inappropriate term, Avesta having extended its meaning from the more ancient texts to all later explanations of those texts in the same language.

The term 'Pahlavi,' or language of Pahlav, next calls for explanation. It is not necessary to investigate its derivation, except to adopt Haug's explanation, that it is connected 'with the Parthva of the Cuneiform Inscriptions, the land of the Parthians known to the Greeks and Romans, and of the Pahlava mentioned by Sanskrit writers.' The change of Parthva into Pahlāv is very similar to that of 'Mithra' into Persian 'Mihr.' In its widest extent, the word 'Pahlavi' is applied to all the varying forms of the mediaeval Persian language, but 'it has long been practically restricted to the written language of Persia during the Sassanian dynasty, and to the literature of that period and a short time after, of which some fragments

[1] S. B. E., vol. v., *Pahlavi Texts*, pt. i. p. x.

[2] Haug's *Essays on the Sacred Language, Writings, and Religion of the Parsis*, p. 120.

have been preserved by the Parsi[1].' Any fragments of Pahlavi composition of later date than A. D. 1000, must be considered merely as modern imitations of a dead language.

'The mediaeval Persian language is only called Pahlavi, when it is written in one of the characters used before the invention of the modern Persian alphabet. . . . Whenever it is transcribed either in Avesta characters or in those of the modern Persian alphabet, it is called Pāzand[2]' (our fourth word that needed explanation).

The word Pāzand, therefore, probably means 're-explanation,' that is, a further interpretation of the Pahlavi-Zand in the Persian vernacular. But the term is applied not only to the purely Persian words in Pahlavi texts, but also (as already noticed) to transliterations of the said texts, either in Avesta or modern Persian characters, in which all obsolete forms are replaced by their Pāzand equivalents. These transliterations form what are called Pāzand texts; and as many as have been examined seem to have been written in India.

But we have not yet fully explained the mysteries of Pahlavi. It is precisely the peculiarity of the language, *when written*, that made its character a standing puzzle to European scholars, until Haug first satisfactorily explained its mode of writing. The key to unlock the door of interpretation lay in the historical Inscriptions. From them it was found that the Persians of Parthian times had, like the Assyrians of old, borrowed their writing from a foreign race; only, these later Aryan Persians accepted a Semitic alphabet, whereas the Semitic Assyrians adopted an Akkadian syllabary. Besides the alphabet, they also transferred a certain number of complete Semitic words to their writings, as representatives of the corresponding words

[1] Haug's *Essays on the Sacred Language, Writings, and Religion of the Parsis*, p. 81.

[2] S. B. E., vol. v. pt. i. p. xii.

in their own language. The number of these might at any time be increased or diminished at the discretion of the writer; but they were probably never very numerous, for not more than four hundred of them are to be found in the Pahlavi writings now extant. These represent nearly all the commonest words in the language, and so often constitute more than half the bulk of a Pahlavi text[1].

Added to the four hundred Semitic logograms already mentioned, we find also about one hundred obsolete forms of Iranian words used as logograms, much in the same way as 'Xmas' may be used for 'Christmas' in English, or 'lb.' for 'pound.' These logograms form what is called the Huzvāriṣ portion of the Pahlavi, while the other words, intended to be pronounced as they are spelt, form the Pāzand portion.

The conclusion, therefore, to which we have come is, that Pahlavi has the appearance of being a compound language. Some of its commonest words are written, either with Semitic letters, or as Semitic words, and a few of its words are written in obsolete Iranian; both of these kinds being called Huzvāriṣ. Other words are either purely Persian, or transliterated from Avesta characters, or from modern Persian characters into Pahlavi; these forms all taking the name of Pāzand. And to add to the general confusion, Persian terminations are often added to Semitic words. As if this were not enough, there are good reasons for supposing that the language was never spoken as it was written.

The Language of the Zend-Avesta.

It has been pointed out by Haug that 'the languages of Persia, commonly called Iranian, form a separate family of the great Aryan stock of languages.' Among Iranian languages proper, he classes

[1] S. B. E., vol. v. pt. i. p. xiii.

the ancient, mediaeval, and modern languages of Irān, in the following way[1]:—

(*a*) The East Iranian or Bactrian branch, extant only in two dialects—the Gātha and the classical Avesta. The former is the more ancient, and is the language of the so-called Gātha or hymns. The latter, in which most of the books of the Zend-Avesta are written, was for many centuries the spoken and written language of Bactria. These Bactrian languages seem to have died out in the third century B.C., leaving no daughters.

(*b*) The West Iranian languages (of Media and Persia), known to us during three periods, but only in the one dialect, which has at every period served as the written language throughout the Iranian provinces of the Persian empire. These three periods of history were—ancient Persia under the Achaemenians (B.C. 500–300); mediaeval Persia under the Arsacidans (B.C. 300–A.D. 226), of whom no records remain; modern Persia under the Sassanians (A.D. 200–600), who have left us many Inscriptions on rocks and coins in the Pahlavi language.

The original language of the Parsi Scriptures, as we have seen already, is not rightly called Zend, and the term should be discarded, as having no reference to a language, but only to commentaries to a language. But, as we have seen, they are written in two dialects of the ancient Bactrian tongue. For want of a better term, we may follow the Parsi scholars in using the term Avesta for the language of the Avesta.

What, then, is the Avesta language, so highly developed and rich in inflexions? It is a sister of Sanskrit, Greek, Latin, and Gothic—no longer in the prime of life, but rather in declining years. Notwithstanding the symptoms of decay, its relation to the most ancient Sanskrit, the so-called Vedic dialect, is as close as that of the different dialects of the Greek

[1] Haug's *Essays*, p. 65 ff.

language to each other (e.g. Æolic, Ionic, Doric, and Attic). So that the languages of the sacred hymns of the Brāhman, and of those of the Parsi, are only the two dialects of two separate tribes of one and the same nation. It is noticeable that it is related closely to Vedic, and not to classical Sanskrit, differences in grammar being very small, and phonetic changes from one to the other very regular.

The two dialects to which we have just referred are found in the language of the Gātha, and in the classical or ordinary Avesta. It is very difficult to decide whether they represent the same language at two different periods of time, or whether they are two contemporary dialects, spoken in two different provinces of the ancient Bactrian empire. If the difference between the Gātha dialect and the Avesta language were only phonetic, it would be reasonable to suppose that they were two different methods of pronunciation, as generally happens in different districts with nations speaking the same language. There are great phonetic changes, and several of these are due to the lengthening of final vowels (e.g. *yā* into *ē-eā*), and these are attributable to the custom of chanting the Gātha. But, besides phonetic, there are decided grammatical changes, so that throughout the Gātha are to be found fuller and older forms of speech, whereas in the Avesta language these forms are later and more contracted.

Judging from these and other peculiarities, there is little doubt that the Gātha date back to a higher antiquity of composition than can be claimed for the ordinary Avesta. But as the differences are not so great as between Vedic and classical Sanskrit, or between the Greek of Homer and the Attic dialect, the Gātha dialect is about two centuries older than the ordinary Avesta language, which was itself the standard language of the ancient Iranian empire under the Achaemenians.

Much of the difficulty of understanding Zend-Avesta

texts arises from the absence of a knowledge of grammar among ancient Persians and Bactrians. This had made the compilation of accurate texts very difficult, and Westergaard has had to take great trouble to give a correct text, according to the oldest MSS. accessible to him. There is still a great need of diffusing a sound and critical knowledge of the Avesta language.

The Original Extent of the Zend-Avesta.

Though the Zend-Avesta in its present state is a comparatively small book, we learn both from ancient classical writers, and from the tradition of the Parsi, that the religious literature of the ancient Persians was of considerable extent. Thus Pliny reports, on the authority of Hermippus the Greek philosopher, that Zoroaster composed two millions of verses; and an Arab historian, Abu Jafir Attavari, assures us that Zoroaster's writings covered twelve hundred cowhides (parchments). Such an extensive ancient literature could only be the work of centuries; for fit writing materials were both scarce and expensive, besides which Orientals require a long time for original composition. They are said to have possessed their whole scripture in the form of twenty-one books, called Nask, each containing Avesta and Zand. Evidently the number twenty-one was an artificial arrangement, in order to have one Nask to each of the twenty-one words of the most sacred formula of the Zoroastrians; and so, each of the Nask was indexed under one particular word of this formula.

Several descriptions of the contents of these Nask are extant, and from them we see clearly that they must represent the whole religious and scientific literature current throughout the ancient Persian empire; for they treated not only of religious topics, but of medicine, astronomy, agriculture, botany, philosophy, &c. These were undoubtedly the books which were known to the Greeks and Romans; and indexes of them, similar to the catalogues of the ancient literature known to Parsi priests nowadays, were extant at the time of Alexander the Great.

The History of the Formation of a Canon.

We have already mentioned the fact of a collection and artificial arrangement of ancient literature, sacred to the Persians, into twenty-one Nask. This was carried out during the Sassanian period, while Zoroastrianism was the state religion. But these Nask were further subdivided into three classes, each containing seven Nask; they were known as the Gātha group (gāsān), the group of the law (dāt), and the group of the Hadha-māthra—what we should respectively call the theological, legal, and mixed groups of writings.

There are two accounts given in the *Dīn-kard*[1], which furnish us with a history of the formation of the Avesta: the one extending from its origin to the time of Alexander, and the other relating to the restoration of the Avesta after the Greek invasion; the first being vague and legendary, while the second is precise and historical. It would be beyond our subject to go into the details of this history, except in the first case, when we are considering the likely date of Zoroaster, the Gātha, and the earlier parts of the Avesta, and in the second, when we are establishing the year in which the Canon was properly closed. All we would do here is to indicate the three occasions on which a collection was made from some old fragments. The first edition to our surprise emanated from a Parthian king, Valkhash; the second from the first Sassanian king, Ardashīr Bābagān (211–241 A.D.); the third and last from King Shāhpūr I (241–272 A.D.)[2].

[1] Prof. Wilson is convinced that the *Dīn-kard* is a modern work (*Parsi Religion*, p. 414).

[2] S. B. E., vol. iv. pt. i. (second edition), p. xxxviii.

The Present Contents of the Zend-Avesta.

The Parsi ascribe the loss of most of their ancient writings, known to the Greeks, mainly to the ravages that followed on the conquest of the Persian empire by Alexander the Great; especially on the occasion of the burning of the citadel and royal palace at Persepolis in a drunken frolic. And, as we know, these facts are mentioned by Western writers. But even if the official copies of the sacred books had been burnt and ravaged, there must have remained other copies of many portions of them; and it was from these scattered copies that the first Sassanian monarchs collected what they did, which was considerable. True, they were chiefly fragments, but some portion of nearly every book seems to have been recovered by them. The total disappearance of most of the books must be traced to recent times, and was due to the later ravages and persecutions of the Mohammedans[1].

What now remain are divided generally into two groups[2]. The *Avesta proper* contains:—

The Vandīdād, a compilation of religious laws and of mythical tales, forming a priestly code;
The Visparad, a collection of litanies for the sacrifice;
The Yasna, a composition of similar litanies and five Gātha (old hymns).

The *Khorda* (or Small) *Avesta* is composed of several short prayers, recited both by the priests and all the faithful at certain times and seasons. These are:—

The five Gāh.
The thirty formulae of Sīrōzah.
The three Āfrigān.
The six Nyāyiṣ.

[1] Haug's *Essays*, pp. 123–125.

[2] S. B. E., vol. iv., *Zend-Avesta* (second edition), pt. i. pp. xxxi, xxxii.

It is also usual to include the Yaṣt, or hymns of praise, and a number of fragments, e.g. the Hadhōkat Nask.

The Avesta proper is found in MSS. in two different forms: either each of the three books are by themselves, in which case they are generally accompanied by a Pahlavi translation; or the three are mingled together according to the requirements of the liturgy. In this case the collection is called the Vandīdād Sāda, or 'Vandīdād pure,' as it exhibits the original text alone without a translation.

What helped to preserve the Avesta is obvious; taken as a whole it does not profess to be a religious encyclopaedia, but only a liturgical collection, and it bears more likeness to our Prayer Book than to our Bible. Thus the Vandīdād Sāda, which had to be recited every day, would be more carefully preserved than the Yaṣt, which are generally recited only once a month. And we are no longer in the dark as to the character and contents of that larger literature of which our Avesta is but a remnant, for it is now known to us in its general outlines through a Pahlavi analysis, which was made in the ninth century—two centuries after the Arab conquest—at a time when the sacred literature of Sassanian times was still in existence[1].

Interpretation of the Zend-Avesta.

There are two distinct methods in use of interpreting the sacred scriptures of the Parsi, called the comparative and the traditional methods. The comparative school hold that the key to the Avesta is the Veda, and not the Pahlavi language. They say that Sanskrit and Avesta are the echoes of one and the same voice, the reflex of one and the same thought, and therefore the Veda form the best lexicon and commentary to the Avesta. They have felt that

[1] S. B. E., vol. iv. pt. i. (second edition), p. xxxiii.

translating the Avesta in accordance with the Pahlavi is not really translating the Avesta, but only the Pahlavi version of it, which is found, wherever deciphered, to wander strangely from the true meaning of the original text; for tradition is wont to force the ideas of its own age into the books of past ages.

The traditional school argue that translating Zand by means of Sanskrit, and Avesta by means of the Veda, is forgetting that relationship is not identity. And the Vedic language is quite unable to teach us what became in Persia of those elements which are common to the two systems. Further, that the comparative method when left to itself leads to wrong conclusions, e.g. the Zand *meregha*, which means 'a bird,' would assume the meaning of 'gazelle,' to accord with the Sanskrit *mṛiga*; and 'the demons,' 'the Daēva,' would ascend from their dwelling in hell up to heaven to meet their philological brothers, the Indian 'Deva.' The fact being that the traditional method starts from matters of fact, and moves always in the field of reality; while the comparative method starts from a hypothesis, moves in a vacuum, and builds up a fanciful religion and a fanciful language.

What really is the case is as follows: tradition discovers and the Veda explains; the former made us acquainted with the nature of the old Iranian religion, by gathering together all its materials; the latter tried to explain its growth; tradition is apt to lose sight of chronological order, and give place to logical order instead; comparison is likely to exaggerate historical allusions from a want of discretion in judgement.

But the question has been ably shown by Professor Darmesteter to be a much wider one than that of pre-historic times. 'In fact,' he says, 'we find in the Avesta either polemics against, or loans from, the great contemporary systems, the Brāhmanical, the Buddhist, the Greek, and the Jewish[1].' These and

[1] S. B. E., vol. iv. (second edition), Introd., p. li.

other elements which have found their way into, or are characteristic of the Avesta, will best be analyzed by a study of the theology and religious teachings of the sacred book itself. But before doing so, it will be well to establish some facts as to its origin and founder.

III.

The Origin and Founder of the Zoroastrian Religion.

'All antiquity,' says De Harlez, 'Iranian as well as Greek, gives it as fact that a philosopher-priest, at an ancient date which is quite uncertain, reformed the creed and worship of Iranian peoples. History calls him Zoroaster. His existence up to the present day was never doubted. Even to-day the majority and the chief among Iranian scholars take him to have been a real person. Others, at the same time, would only have him pictured as a legendary being, representing the body of Mazdean priests. One has even transformed him into a god of storms[1].' But it requires very strong proof to upset the unanimous voice of classical antiquity. On the whole, therefore, we take it that he actually existed.

The age in which Zoroaster lived is by no means certain. After a close investigation of Oriental and Western writings, Geiger and Spiegel have been unable to determine the period accurately. For Oriental authorities are quite unreliable upon this point, for they say that 'Zoroaster belongs to the middle portion of the duration of the world since the creation of the human race, or 9,000 years after the creation of the world.' They also state dogmatically that 'a thousand years cannot yet have fully elapsed since his death, for otherwise a new prophet should have already appeared.' Among Western writers, 'Xanthus of Sardis is said to have placed Zoroaster 600 years before the fall of Xerxes.' In

[1] C. de Harlez, *Avesta*, Introd., p. xviii.

this case, 'he must have flourished about 1080 years before Christ.' Eudoxus, Aristotle, and Hermodorus fix absurd dates, while Hermippus, Pliny, and Plutarch are just as indefinite. Berosus, Porphyrius, and Agathias are scarcely more trustworthy, and Suidas and Ktesias not reliable.

Again, the birthplace and native country of Zoroaster are not decided upon. Ktesias has been followed by many other later historians in assigning Bactria as his native home. But a whole series of authorities look upon him as a Mede or a Persian. Amongst them is to be found Berosus, who held a great character for accuracy in ancient times. Turning to Oriental writers once again, they unanimously place Zoroaster in Western Irān as his native land, but most of them state that he had worked for some time in Bactria. The Avesta speaks of him as 'the renowned in the Aryan home,' wherever that may be. The Bundahish definitely assigns his birthplace to be near the river 'Darja, in the Aryan home.' From the above conflicting statements we can only say that most writers try to place the native land of Zoroaster altogether in the West and not in the East[1].

The Zoroastrian Theology before Alexander the Great.

We have historical evidence of some essential doctrines in Zoroastrianism, the existence of which can be traced back far beyond the Parthian period and the Greek conquest. One may with certain accuracy distinguish in the religion what is old (or pre-Alexandrian, or Achaemenian) from what is late (or post-Alexandrian)[2].

I. The belief in a supreme God, Ahura-Mazda, who is the organizer of the world, is as old as anything we know about Persia. Darius proclaims Auramazda,

[1] Spiegel, *Age of the Avesta and Zoroaster*, pp. 82 ff.
[2] S. B. E., vol. iv. (second edition), pp. lx ff.

the greatest of all gods, a powerful God, who made this earth, who made that heaven, who made man, who made Darius king.

II. The gods invoked with the Persian Zeus (Auramazda) are, according to Herodotus, the Sun, the Moon, the Earth, the Wind, the Waters, that is to say, natural deities. The two greatest gods, next to him, according to Artaxerxes Memnon, are Mithra and Anahata (Anāhita), that is to say, a God of the Light, and a Goddess of the Waters.

III. The principle of Dualism is implied, in the time of Darius, by the great king stating that Ahura 'created welfare (shiyātim) for man'; and in the time of Herodotus, by the religious war waged by the Magi against the ants, snakes, and other noxious creatures, which shows that the distinction of Ormazdian and Ahrimanian creatures was already in existence. Moreover, at the end of the Achaemenian period, Aristotle knows of a Good Spirit and the Evil One, Zeus (Oromazdes) and Ades (Areimanios).

IV. The existence of the World was limited to twelve thousand years, distributed into four periods, the character of which was altered in the post-Alexandrian period, to humour the Neo-Platonic tendencies of the age. It was already an established dogma that Ahriman would be conquered at last, and that men should live again. The belief in resurrection and a future life implies the correlative belief in future rewards and punishments, which was fully developed later on.

V. Practical morality was already a trait in the national character. Truthfulness was considered a paramount virtue; the doctrine of the balance of merits and demerits was already known. The two greatest merits of a citizen in the days of Darius and Herodotus, as now, were the begetting and rearing of a numerous family, and the fruitful tilling of the soil.

VI. The worship of the elements—water, fire, and earth—and a respect for purity were practised. For it was forbidden to sully the waters or the fire, to throw a corpse into the fire, or to bury it in the earth until reduced to a fleshless, incorruptible skeleton.

VII. Two sorts of sacrifice existed — the bloody sacrifice, as seen to-day in the Ātashzōhr, and the bloodless sacrifice, consisting essentially of the Haoma-offering and libations, of which we have indirect evidence.

The principles of the Achaemenian religion may be summed up as follows:—

I. Dogmas: the existence of two conflicting supreme powers, one good and the other evil, Ormazd and Ahriman; the final defeat of Ahriman after twelve thousand years; and the resurrection; also a number of Animistic deities, amongst which were Mithra and Anāhita.

II. Morals: veneration of truth, family, and agriculture.

III. Liturgy: a bloody sacrifice and a bloodless sacrifice (Haoma); certain laws of purity extending to the waters, the fire, and the earth; burning and burying corpses forbidden.

The Magi.

This religion was practised in the south as well as in the north of Irān, in Persia as well as in Media. It had its centre in Media, and its sacerdotal class belonged to a Median tribe, the Magi. The priesthood was hereditary—as it still is nowadays amongst the Parsi—and the Magi were to Mazdeism what the Levites and Cohenim were to Judaism. The sacerdotal tribe spread wherever Mazdeism extended; and in spite of the intense provincial hatred which the Persians bore to the Medians, still the Magi were, in the Persian idea, the only true, authorized priests.

Aryan Elements.

Purely Aryan elements in the religion are:—the supreme God, the God of the Heaven, Ahura-Mazda; the God of the heavenly light, Mithra; the worship of the elementary divinities, Waters, Fire, and Earth; a number of storm-myths and mythical legends; and the worship of Haoma.

Iranian Elements.

Purely Iranian elements are:—the dualistic conception of the world, and its limited duration of twelve thousand years with its four periods; the continual conflict of Ormazd and Ahriman, and the latter's defeat; the resurrection of the dead, the notion of purity carried to the extreme, the prohibition of burning or burying the dead, and the throwing away of corpses to dogs and birds of prey.

Some of the new dogmas may be the independent development of Aryan elements; for instance, the dualistic conception may have grown out of the mythical struggles between gods and demons. But the Great year and the resurrection are things quite new, which seem to betray external influences. But whether these influences were Scythian or Chaldean it is difficult to decide.

IV.

The Ritual of the Zend-Avesta.

There are four leading features in the ritual of the Parsis, as outlined in the Avesta—the care of the sacred fire, special forms of prayer, offerings, and purification.

There are two classes of fire-temples, the seven 'Ātash Bahrams,' and over a hundred 'Ātash Adarans.' There is no common worship, but the priests keep a continual watch over the sacred fire, so that it never goes out, feeding it with sandal-wood and gum benzoin.

This fire is kept in a shrine, within an outer court, where the people praying can always see its light, and it burns in a large urn on a stone altar. The priest sits within the shrine when praying, facing the fire and cross-legged, holding in his left hand the 'barsom,' now made of silver rods.

It is specially during the recitation of prayers that the barsom is used. These prayers are chanted at different times of the day, every portion having its allotted prayer. They are generally pronounced without being understood, because they are Zand prayers in the Gūjarati character.

As regards offerings, the old animal sacrifices of Achaemenian times have practically ceased, and even in the normal offering 'the flesh' is no longer used and offered. The only part of the offering still observed is the libation of the sacred plant of Haoma, known to the Brāhman as Soma. It is pounded first in the sacred mortar, then the juice is collected in the sacred cup. When accompanied by proper prayers in the process of preparation, 'this liquid becomes endowed with almost divine attributes'!

Lastly, ceremonial purity is with the Parsi a matter of supreme importance, though the distinction between moral and ceremonial defilement is far from clear in the Avesta. The one is regarded as equally dreadful with the other, and as requiring equal expiation. The chief means of purification are water and 'gomez,' or 'nirang,' which must be properly prepared and applied with prayers. As Anquetil tersely puts it, there is 'no purification, no purifier, no priest, and no Parsi.' Every morning the orthodox Parsi, with a view to purification, applies the nirang to his face, hands, and feet, after saying his prayers; the liquid is even drunk on greater occasions, pomegranate-leaves being chewed to banish the taste. The greatest of all purifications is the Barashnūm, a ceremony which lasts in all for nine nights, and always precedes the ordination of the priest.

Birth, Marriage, and Burial Ceremonies.

Four other ceremonies connected with the Parsi between birth and burial call for notice. To inculcate humility a Parsi must be born on the ground floor, and washed with water before being considered pure. On the seventh day the astrologer is called in to name the child and divine his future. Nowadays at the age of seven, or later, the rite of initiation into Zoroastrianism takes place. It is accompanied by prayers, purifications, and the putting on of the 'kusti' (or sacred cord of seventy-two threads) and the 'sadara' (or sacred shirt). These must be worn day and night without fail.

At the age of fifteen marriage is permitted, though earlier marriages are not at all infrequent. The priest is the matchmaker, and the astrologer fixes the day for marriage. Cloth and twist unite the couple, followed by prayers and the dastur's blessing. Their home at first is with the bridegroom's father; and, unlike Hindū widows, Parsi widows are allowed to marry again.

Lastly, in death and burial Parsi ceremonies are unique. Their sense of defilement through contact with anything dead has led to elaborate ceremonies. When a Parsi is dying, the priest repeats consoling texts from the Avesta, administers the sacred cup of Haoma, and prays for the forgiveness of his sins. After death, the body is removed to the ground floor and prepared for burial. Priestly exhortations then begin, during which a white dog, 'four-eyed,' is brought in to gaze upon the dead and thus expel the demon, and secure the passage of the soul over the Chinvat bridge to heaven.

The same day the body is conveyed to the 'tower of silence,' or *dakhma*, by a special class of Parsi. Within the *dakhma* the corpses are exposed to the birds of prey, till only the skeleton remains. This grim practice is thus described in the Avesta in a golden light[1]:

> 'O Maker of the material world, thou Holy One!
> Whither shall we bring, where shall we lay the bones of the dead, O Ahura-Mazda?'

Ahura-Mazda answered[1]:

> 'The worshippers of Mazda shall erect a building out of the reach of the dog, of the fox, and of the wolf, and wherein rain-water cannot stay. Such a building shall they erect, if they can afford it, with stones, mortar, and earth (?); if they cannot afford it, they shall *lay down the dead man on the ground*, on his carpet and his pillow, *clothed with the light of heaven*, and *beholding the sun*.'

V.

The Mohammedan Conquest of Persia.

The Sassanian dynasty was at the height of its power by the time the Canon of the Avesta was closed, under Adarbād Mahraspand, in the reign of Shāhpūr II (330 A.D.). It now remains for us to sketch the events that led the Parsi to migrate to India. We will begin by describing how the kingdom of Persia passed into Arab hands.

The first invasion began by order of Caliph Omar in 633 A.D. But it was the great Arab victories at Kādisīya (in that memorable year 637 A.D.) and Nahāvand (probably 641 A.D.) that shattered the remains of the Sassanian empire. When the country had been finally subjugated, the Caliphate was established at Baghdad, and the nation was compelled by the soldiery of Omar to accept death or the Koran. 'A hundred thousand persons are said to have been forced daily to abjure the faith of their forefathers; and the fire-temples and other sacred places were destroyed or converted into mosques. Under rulers carrying out this system without pity or remorse, almost the whole Zoroastrian population of Persia embraced the faith of Islām. Such of the followers of Zoroaster as obeyed the dictates of their conscience abandoned their homes and fled to the mountainous districts of Khorassan.

[1] S. B. E., vol. iv. pt. i. pp. 73, 74.—*Vandīdād*, vi. 49-51.

For about a hundred years they remained in Khorassan unmolested, but persecution at last reached them, and they were once more compelled to flee. A considerable number succeeded in reaching the little island of Ormuz, at the entrance of the Persian Gulf[1].'

Emigration to India.

Then came the migration to India, first (so the story goes) by sea to Diu, off the south of the Kathiawar coast, then nineteen years later to Sanjan, where they landed about the year 716 A.D. Here the first fire-temple was allowed to be built in India. Hence they are traced to Cambay (A.D. 942–997), and to Variav about the same time; also to Surat and other places in the north, and Thana and Chaul in the south, of Western India; also to the city of Navsari by 1142 A.D., and Anklesvar a century later. It was in the last-named place that the Visparad is said to have been translated in 1258 A.D. Mention is also made of a 'dakhma' being built at Broach in 1309 A.D.

Travellers in India of the fourteenth, fifteenth, and sixteenth centuries found the Parsi in many parts of the country. And we know that in the fourteenth century they were persecuted by the Mohammedans, and had to move their sacred fire from Sanjan to Navsari, which is now considered by them to be a very sacred spot. Not much can be chronicled during the centuries of Mohammedan supremacy, but we find them in the Mogul city of Surat in 1478 A.D., and can be fairly certain that they first arrived in Bombay shortly before the cession of the island to the British in 1668 A.D.

Population, Mortality, and Occupations.

The last Indian census (of 1891) numbered the Parsi in India at 89,904, or an increase of a little over five per cent. in ten years. This represents about

[1] Dosabha Sorabji Karaka, *History of the Parsis*, vol. i. p. 22 ff.

one three-thousandth part of the entire population, but no less than one-fifteenth of the population of the city of Bombay. The great vitality of the nation is shown by the fact that Parsi families have the highest average number of children under one year of age. This will best be brought out by the comparative table below.

Death rate under one year of age.

Jaina . . .	54·47 %	Brāhman . .	20·4 %
Hindū Sūdra .	33·6 %	European . .	20·18 %
Mohammedan	30·46 %	Parsi . . .	19·26 %
Hindū . . .	26·11 %		

The Parsi are essentially men of the towns, and not masters of estates. Not a single Parsi appears returned by the census as a soldier, for the simple reason that he can always get a higher salary than a sepoy by other occupations. They are mostly occupied with educational, commercial, and industrial pursuits, and none are found in the menial occupations of life. Mendicancy is almost unknown among them, and no nation on earth has a greater regard for chastity of life.

Costumes.

The Parsi have given up the dress of their co-religionists in Persia, and wear costumes somewhat similar to the Hindū, and adapted to the climate. Children only wear a single garment—in the form of a loose shirt of cotton, flannel, or silk, called 'jabhla,' which reaches from neck to knee—until the age of seven. Lately light trousers have been introduced among the upper classes. The 'topi' on the head, and shoes on the feet, complete the costume. Boys and girls are dressed alike, except that girls wear long hair and ornaments, especially earrings.

The Parsi at home wears a long muslin shirt and girdle, a waistcoat of white cloth with sleeves, loose cotton trousers, slippers, and a China-silk skull-cap. When going out, he puts on his turban, of dark chocolate colour, over the skull-cap, unless he be a priest, and then he wears a white turban. He also wears an 'angrakha,' or loose overcoat, with very long sleeves that roll up above the wrist. For full dress he needs a 'jama' or a long, double-breasted coat of cotton, and a piece of cloth, which is folded in bands, and passed again and again round the waist. This dress is worn at weddings, funerals, and on certain state occasions.

The Parsi women wear similar underclothing to the men. But their 'sari' or outer dress is composed of about six yards of bright-coloured silk or satin. This is most gracefully arranged round the waist, limbs, and shoulders. Besides this, the old-fashioned 'kanchri' has been generally superseded by a bodice made after the English fashion. Every one except a widow wears glass bangles, and until a generation or so ago nose-rings were worn also. The old tradition that the head should be covered day and night is kept by the women wearing their 'mathatana,' under which, for modesty's sake, all their hair is secreted. For the same reason the men always wear their skull-caps. But every year Western ideas are prevailing more amongst them.

Parsi Sects and the Calendar.

The Parsi of India are divided into two sects, the Shehenshai and the Kadmi. They differ, not on questions of faith, but of chronology. Both have their own computation of the era of Yazdezard, the last Sassanian king. The division amongst them arose in this way:—The Parsi reckon a year to have 365 days, and a month thirty days; so that every year they add five days, or Gātha, at the close. In order to make up the 5 h. 54 m., and so accord with the correct solar year, the ancient Persians are reported to have intercalated 'one month' at the end of every 120 years. This intercalation is called Kabisa. Now the Persian Zoroastrians seem to have forgotten to make this intercalation after they lost the sovereignty of the land; and so when one Jamasp, a learned Persian Zoroastrian, arrived in Surat in 1090 A.D. to instruct the 'mobeds' or priests, he discovered that his co-religionists in India were a month behind their brethren in Irān in commencing the new year. But it was not till 1746 A.D. that the Kadmi sect was formed to observe the same dates as the Persian Zoroastrians. The bulk of the people then became Shehenshai, and adhered to their old traditions. Quite an ardent controversy was then started, and not cleared up until Kharsedji Rastamji Kama published his work on the computation of the Yazdezardi era (in 1870). Though a Kadmi, he showed that both sects were curiously in the wrong; for the Kadmi erred in saying that intercalation was not enjoined by the Zoroastrian religion, and the Shehenshai were wrong, inasmuch as no intercalation had taken place (as they supposed) when the Parsi refugees were in Khorassan.

A special feature about the Parsi calendar is the great stress laid upon the importance of each day for different things. For instance, the first day of the month is the right day to enter a new house or garden; other days are best for a journey or a voyage; others for social gatherings; while some are reserved for rest and pious contemplation[1]. But it is not necessary to add that the Parsi no longer follow the above precepts as laid down by the fertile brain of Ādarbād.

Festivals.

There are several Parsi festivals still widely observed.

Perhaps the most appreciated of all is the Pateti holiday. *Pateti,* or New Year's Day, is the day of

[1] Dosabhai Sorabji Karaka, *History of the Parsis*, vol. i. ch. iii. pp. 133–143.

Ahura-Mazda in the month of Fravardin, which should properly be called Naoroz.

Rapithvan is the third day of the first month, and originally was intended to announce the commencement of summer.

Khordad-Lal marks the anniversary of the birth of their prophet Zoroaster.

Besides these and other holidays, there are the *six Gahambar*, or days of rest. The Zoroastrian theory that the world was created in 365 days, at six unequal intervals, has occasioned the observance of the Gahambar. The good old custom of rich and poor, high and low, partaking of food together and uniting in prayers, is still observed at these times.

Parsi Law and Government.

There is no record of the laws by which the Parsi were first governed when they arrived in India. But journeys were subsequently made to Persia, with the result that the Arda-vīraf-nama, the Viṣtasp Yaṣt, and the Visparad were brought back from Persia, and long acted as guides on religious and social questions.

A properly constituted Panchayat was first formed in Bombay soon after the island passed into British hands. In religious matters the priests of Navsari did and still do hold their own, but civil disputes were all settled by this court of justice. Its decision was considered as final. But this state of things only lasted till the middle of the eighteenth century, when it was further decided by the British governor, owing to pending troubles, that the Panchayat should form 'a general assembly' of the Parsi. During the lifetime of the first-appointed members the assembly was very powerful, but then it gradually declined and fell into contempt. Again it regained its power, and again it declined, chiefly owing to the injustice of having 'one law for the rich and another for the poor.' Its only function now consists in being trustee to certain Parsi charitable funds.

For some time the Parsi remained with no code of laws, but merely subject to the common Hindū law, to which they had subscribed on their first landing at Sanjan centuries ago. But a Parsi Law Commission was established, and finally succeeded in securing laws for the Parsi from the British Government.

CHAPTER II

THE JAINA

'He that hateth his life (ψυχη) *in this world shall keep it unto life eternal.'*—St. John, xii. 25.

I. Their present extent and social importance—Discovery of their origin—Mahāvīra, the twenty-fourth Jīna—Mahāvīra a contemporary and rival to Buddha—Parallels and contrasts—The influence of Gōsāla—Brāhmanism, Buddhism, and Jainism—Their relationship—Jainism not a Buddhist sect—Jaina, Buddhist, and Brāhman vows compared—Jainism a development of Brāhmanism—The institution of the fourth Āsrama—Views on the Ātman.

II. Authenticity of Jaina tradition—The Mathurā Inscriptions—The age of Jaina literature—Date of Devarddhi and the Jaina Canon—Date of composition of the Siddhānta—Tests of scientific knowledge, by language and spelling of the texts, and by the metres used—Works older than the existing Canon—The Pūrva—Contents of the Siddhānta.

III. Antiquity of Jaina philosophy—Early Jaina doctrines: The eternity of Atman; the kriyāvāda; the annihilation of Karman; the three daṇḍa; the doctrine of kātuyāma saṃvarasamvutō—Early religious practices of Nigaṇṭha—Leading Jaina doctrines of to-day—Jiva and Ajīva—Moksha—The Jaina worship and temples.

The Jaina of To-day.

THE Jaina, who are the most numerous and influential sect of nonconformists to the Brāhmanical system of Hindūism, now number about 1,400,000 in India. They are found in every province of Upper Hindustan, in the cities along the Ganges, and in Calcutta. But they are more numerous to the west, e. g. in Rajputāna, Gūjarat, and in the upper part of the Malabar coast. They are also scattered throughout the whole of Southern India. Being mostly traders, merchants, or bankers, they live in the towns, and the wealth of many of their community gives them a social importance greater than would result from their mere numbers. It is even said that half the mercantile transactions of India pass through their hands. Their charity is boundless; and they form the chief supporters of the beast hospitals, which the old and striking animistic tenderness for animals has left in many of the cities of India.

Discovery of their Origin.

Until quite recently European scholars did not admit the pretensions of the Jaina to an earlier origin than Buddhism. H. H. Wilson questioned their importance at any period earlier than twelve centuries ago [1]. Weber used to regard 'the Jaina as merely one of the oldest sects of Buddhism [2]'; and Lassen believed that they had branched off from the Buddhists [3]. M. Barth, after discussion of the evidence, still thought that we must regard the Jaina 'as a sect which took its rise in Buddhism [4].' On the other hand, Oldenberg, who brings later light from the Pāli texts to bear on the question, accepts the identity of the Jaina sect with the Nigaṇṭha, 'into whose midst the younger brotherhood of Buddha entered [5].'

The learned Jacobi has now investigated the question from the Jaina texts themselves. Oldenberg had proved, out of the Buddhist Scriptures, that Buddhism was a true product of Brāhman doctrine and discipline. Jacobi shows that both 'Buddhism and Jainism must be regarded as religions developed

[1] *Essays and Lectures on the Religion of the Hindus*, by H. H. Wilson. Dr. Reinhold Rost's edition (1862), vol. i. p. 329.

[2] Weber's *Indische Studien*, xvi. 210.

[3] Lassen's *Indische Alterthumskunde*, iv. 763 ff.

[4] Barth's *Religions of India*, ed. 1882, p. 151.

[5] *Buddha, his Life, his Doctrine, his Order*, by Professor H. Oldenberg.

out of Brāhmanism, not by a sudden reformation, but prepared by a religious movement going on for a long time.' And he has brought forward evidence for believing that Jainism was the earlier outgrowth of the two—evidence which will be more fully discussed later on. He holds that the religion of the Jaina was probably founded by Pārsvanāth, now revered as the twenty-third Jīna; and merely reformed by Mahāvīra, the contemporary of Buddha.

Following the line of argument that Professor Jacobi has adopted, except where it appears to be somewhat inadequate, we come first to the claims of Mahāvīra to be the founder of Jainism and a contemporary of Buddha.

Mahāvīra, the Twenty-fourth Jīna.

It is now recognized by all scholars that Nātaputta, who is commonly called Mahāvīra or Vardhamāna, was a historical person and a contemporary of Sākyaṃuni, the Buddha; and that the religion of Jainism which he founded is as old as Buddhism. In fact, both took their rise in that wonderful era of religious speculation upon the ultimate problems of life, about the sixth century before Christ; and we would remark that in no other age and country do we find diffused among all classes of people so earnest a spirit of inquiry, so impartial and deep a respect for all who came forward as teachers, however contradictory their doctrines might be.

We see then at once that it is most important to compare Mahāvīra with Buddha, and Buddhism with Jainism, in order to see whether they borrowed any of their teachings from each other, or derived their doctrines, their orders, and their speculations from a common source. In any case, it will be well to note how it was that 'Buddhism proved more adaptable and appealed to more widespread sympathies, till it surpassed and overshadowed Jainism'; still more interesting to trace the cause of the survival of the latter in British India to-day, while the former has long been extinct.

Mahāvīra and Buddha [1].

The chief points of resemblance between the respective founders of these religions were these:—(1) both were ascetics; (2) Mahāvīra had relations with the same names as those of Buddha, both leaders being of the Kshatriya caste; (3) both disregarded the authority of the Brāhmans in religious matters.

But their differences were far more characteristic than their apparent resemblance, of which so much used to be made. For we read of Buddha as being born in Kapilavastu in the kingdom of Magadha at the foot of the Himālaya. But Mahāvīra was the son of one King Siddhānta of Kundagrāma, not far from Vaiṣālī. And Buddha's mother died directly after his birth, but the parents of Mahāvīra lived until he was grown up.

Again, amid the halo of legends that gathered about Buddha's life, we are probably right in saying that he turned an ascetic against his father's will. Who has not been touched by the story of 'the four sights which powerfully affected him, and actually decided his future course? The first object was a decrepit old man: this led him to reflect on the miseries of old age. He next passed a wretched leper, covered with sores: here Gautama's thoughts glanced off to the manifold forms of disease and suffering with which the world abounds. The next object which crossed his path was a dead body; "And this," said he, "is the end to which I and all must come!" . . . Anon, another object presented itself to him: he beheld a recluse sitting rapt in meditation. "That," said he to himself, "is the only course for me to pursue." . . . That very night did he quit his home.' Not so with Mahāvīra,

[1] S. B. E., vol. xxii., *Gaina-Sūtras*, pt. i. p. xiii ff.

for he waited until his father's death, and then went into retirement with the consent of those in power.

But the striking parallels and contrasts go further than this. Whereas Buddha led a life of austerities for six years, Mahāvīra persevered for twelve; and even afterwards, when he became a Tīrthakara, he was still convinced of the necessity of asceticism, whereas Buddha looked upon those six years as wasted time. Thus, after a lifetime of mutual rivalry, Mahāvīra is said to have died at Pāpā, leaving Buddha the advantage of preaching and teaching for many years after, until his touching death at Kusinagara when eighty years of age.

Mahāvīra, like Buddha, was a member of a feudal aristocracy, whose family ties were strong and long remembered. We know, too, for certain, that Buddha addressed himself chiefly to members of the aristocracy, and the Jaina originally preferred the Kshatriya to the Brāhmans. Therefore it is evident that both Buddha and Mahāvīra made use of their families to propagate their order, which partly accounts for their prevalence at the time over rival sects. Then when it is remembered that the kingdom of Magadha was extended under Agaṣatru, son of Bambisāra, who figures largely in the life of Buddha —extended so as to include Vaiṣālī, and the birthplace of Mahāvīra—we see that the foundations were laid of an empire, which facilitated the rapid spread both of Jainism and Buddhism[1].

A few other points about the founder of Jainism are worthy of notice. After he had spent his twelve years in austerities, during eleven of which he seems to have gone about naked, he became omniscient, and a prophet of the Jaina, called a Tīrthakara. Several other titles were then given him, such as Jīna, Mahāvīra, &c. (as with Sākya-muni). Then for thirty years he taught his religious system and organized

[1] S. B. E., vol. xxii. pt. i. p. xiv.

his order of ascetics, under the patronage of the three kings of Videha, Magadha, and Aṅga. His travels extended west to Srāvastī and north to the foot of the Himālaya. His disciples (or apostles of the Jaina) were eleven in number, and are detailed in the Kalpa-Sūtra. This list, we have reason to believe, is accurate, since it is given without variation by both sects of the Jaina. Lastly, we have the double testimony of both Jaina and Buddhist Canons that Nātaputta (as he is always called by the Buddhists) was a contemporary of Buddha, and that his followers in Vaiṣālī were numerous [1].

The Influence of Gōsāla on Mahāvīra's Doctrines.

The Bhagavāti states that Gōsāla, the son of Makkhali, after six years of asceticism with Mahāvīra as his disciple, separated from him and started a Law of his own, and set up a Jīna, the leader of the Āġīvika. The Buddhists claim Gōsāla as coming from a long-established order of monks. Jacobi thinks that Mahāvīra and Gōsāla associated with the intention of combining their sects and fusing them into one. This does not seem conclusive.

His reasons are:—(1) their long life together presupposes similarity of opinions; (2) the divisions of animals, and of mankind, into six classes are common to both; (3) the rules of conduct prove almost conclusively that Mahāvīra borrowed them from Gōsāla.

Certainly Mahāvīra's position was strengthened by his temporary association with Gōsāla, though, if we believe the Jaina, Gōsāla himself lost by it, and came to a tragic end [2].

Brāhmanism, Buddhism, and Jainism.

We have already mentioned that it has been generally believed, even by many scholars, that Jainism is a branch of Buddhism. Let us now ex-

[1] S. B. E., vol. xxii. pt. i. p. xvi. [2] Ibid., vol. xlv. pt. ii. p. xxix ff.

amine the four points of coincidence which Professor Lassen adduced to prove this point [1].

I. Both sects give the same titles and epithets to their prophets: e.g. Jīna, Arhat, Mahāvīra, Śarvagna, Sugata, Tathāgata, Siddha, Buddha, Sambuddha, Parṁivṛita, Mukta.

To this it has been well replied that probably all were 'honorific adjectives and substantives applicable to persons of exalted virtue.' For instance, even to-day in Jaina writings, 'Buddha' means 'mukta,' or 'liberated soul,' and yet it was taken by the Buddhists as a title for Gautama. And to go further, Tīrthakara, which means 'prophet' with the Jaina, is used of the founder of a heretical sect by the Buddhists. The more natural conclusion, therefore, to arrive at is that Buddhists were opponents of Jaina when they formed their terminology, and not vice versa.

II. Both sects now worship mortal men (their prophets) as gods, and erect statues of them in their temples.

But, we answer, this worship had nothing to do with Buddhism or Jainism originally, nor did it originate with the 'yati' or monks, but with the 'srāvaki' or laymen of the community. The religious development of the people in India had come to find in 'bhakti' the supreme means of salvation, and so Professor Jacobi thinks that both sects came to adopt this practice, independently, under the continuous and irresistible religious tendencies at work in those times.

III. Both sects measure the history of the world by enormous periods of time, which bewilder and awe even the most imaginative fancy.

But so does the Brāhman; in fact, there is as much difference between Buddhist and Jaina chronology as

[1] *Indische Alterthumskunde*, iv. 763 ff.

between Buddhist and Brāhman. A study of the three systems seems to show that while 'the Buddhists have improved on the Brāhman system of the Yuga, the Jaina invented their Utsarpiṇī and Avasarpiṇī eras after the model of the day and night of Brahmā.' In this case, therefore, the Jaina outdo the Buddhists.

IV. Both sects lay stress on the 'ahiṇsā' or not killing of living things.

This point refers to only one of the five vows of the Jaina and Buddhists, which have so much in common. It will be best, therefore, to compare these vows with one another, as Professor Weber has done, and underneath to place the first five of the ten obligations of the Brāhman ascetics, as drawn up by Professor Windisch.

The five Jaina vows in order.	*The five Buddhist precepts.*
ahiṇsā, not to destroy life.	One should not destroy life.
sūnṛita, not to lie [1].	One should not take that which is not given [1].
asteya, not to take that which is not given.	One should not tell lies.
brahmakarya, to abstain from sexual intercourse.	One should not become a drinker of intoxicants.
aparigraha, to renounce all interest in worldly things, and to call nothing one's own [2].	One should refrain from unlawful sexual intercourse . . . an ignoble thing [2].

The five vows of the Brāhman ascetics.

Abstention from injuring living beings.
Truthfulness [1].
Abstention from appropriating the property of others.
Continence.
Liberality [2].

[1] Note the change in order.

[2] The fifth vow differs in each case, liberality not being possible for mendicants.

A mere glance at the above triple group of vows is enough to convince any candid inquirer, that there is quite as much reason to suppose that Jaina vows are deducible from those of Brāhman ascetics already in use, as that Buddhism is the source. It is still more obvious when the precepts and rules of the Brāhman ascetics, as in Baudhāyana, are arranged alongside of those of the Jaina monks. They have much the same outfit. Both carry a cloth for straining water, and both perform purifications with water when taken out of a tank and strained. The Brāhman broom has its counterpart in the grasses with which the Jaina sweep the road, where they walk and sit, in order to remove insects. While the stick and the rope belonging to the alms-bowl, the alms-bowl, and the water-vessel are the invariable accompaniments of each. In fact, the only speciality of the Jaina is their filter for the mouth, which they call 'mukhavastrika.' On the whole, therefore, the Jaina were fitted out very much like their Brāhman models, the Saṃnyāsin or Bhikshu. They have more vows in common with the Brāhmans than the Buddhists, and several precepts in common with Brāhman ascetics.

There is still another question to decide. Did the Jaina monk copy from the Brāhman ascetic, or vice versa? That the former is the case has overwhelming evidence. For, putting aside for a moment the claims of the Saṃnyāsin to be part of the Āṣrama, which are probably as old as Brāhmanism itself, we find traces of Brāhman ascetics all over India, at a time when Buddhism was only 200 years old, and still exercising merely a local influence. Therefore it is difficult to conceive how all the Saṃnyāsin could have been taken from the Buddhists.

But still more conclusive is the argument from the date of Gautama, the lawgiver. For Professor Bühler[1] puts down Baudhāyana as of a much older date than the Āpastamba, which we know was written in the

[1] *Sacred Laws of the Āryas*, pt. i. Introduction, p. xliii.

fourth or fifth century B. C. But Gautama was older than either of these, and yet in his day he taught the complete system of Brāhman asceticism.

What then gave rise to the monastic orders of Jaina and Buddhists? It must be remembered that though these orders were copied, as we have seen, from the Brāhmans, they were distinctly intended for the Kshatriya caste, of whom both Mahāvīra and Buddha were members. This is proved by a curious legend about the transfer of the embryo of Mahāvīra from the womb of a Brāhmaṇī to that of a Kshatriyāṇi. For it was alleged that no other caste was worthy to bring forth a Tīrthakara. Now it was only natural that Brāhman ascetics should not regard these fellow-ascetics as quite their equals, however orthodox they might be; and that further separation between them should ensue, when it came to be held that the Brāhman was entitled to enter *the fourth Āṣrama* (or stage), the Kshatriya only three, the citizen two, and the Sūdra one. A remark of Vaisishṭha throws light upon this tendency to dissent, when he deplores the fact that non-Brāhman ascetics had ceased from reciting the Veda, and hence were neglecting revelation. We can be safe in saying that the beginnings of dissenting sects like the Jaina and Buddhists arose out of the institution of the fourth Āṣrama [1].

But there were other differences of belief taking shape in this age of inquiry [2]. The Brāhman philosophy of the *Ātman*, or Universal Soul, was being disputed. And while the Jaina held to the orthodox belief in 'the absolute and permanent soul'—with but one difference, that they ascribed to the Ātman a limited space—Buddha went further. 'The very first sermon which he preached to his first converts (was a) discourse on the absence of any sign of "soul," in any of all the constituent elements of individual life [3].'

[1] S. B. E., vol. xxii. pp. xxix ff.

[2] Cf. p. 58.

[3] T. W. Rhys-Davids, *Buddhism, its History and Literature*, p. 39.

At length, therefore, we have arrived at some conclusions about the relationships between Brāhmanism, Buddhism, and Jainism, and it will be well here to summarize them. *First*, that which Buddhists and Jaina have in common, comes in every case from older Brāhman sources. *Second*, in fundamental points the Buddhists and the Jaina are at variance. *Third*, Mahāvīra and Buddha were undoubtedly contemporaries one of another.

II.

The Authenticity of Jaina Tradition.

The above discussion has, however, been conducted on the supposition that the tradition of the Jaina as contained in their sacred books may on the whole be credited. But the intrinsic value of this tradition has been called into question by M. Barth, who is a scholar of cautious judgement. In his opinion, the direct tradition of peculiar doctrines and records had not yet been demonstrated, and he would seem when he wrote to assume that the Jaina must have been careless in handing down their sacred lore [1]. Professor Weber also concludes the introduction to his recent work by saying, 'Personally I still continue to regard the Jaina as one of the oldest of the Buddhist sects [2].'

A conclusive answer then must be given, before proceeding further, to the question :—'Was the cultivation of the sacred text altogether abandoned in the interval between the days of Mahāvīra and the redaction of the Canon in 454 A.D.?' In answer to Barth's doubts about the authenticity of Jaina traditions, Jacobi admits that the Jaina sect may have been for a long time small and unimportant, but contends that small sects, like the Jews and the Parsi,

[1] Barth, *The Religions of India*, ch. iv (1882 ed.).
[2] Weber, *Sacred Literature of the Jains*, p. 12.

often do preserve their doctrines and traditions with great pertinacity, and better than larger religious communities. He points out that the trifling differences in doctrines and usages which caused the various schisms in the Jaina body, indicate that they were most particular about their tenets, and that the detailed list of teachers and schools in the Sthaviravāli of the Kalpa-Sūtra, which cannot be a pure fabrication, shows the interest taken in the preservation of records. With respect to the sacred books of the Śvetāmbara, he rejects a portion of the tradition, which says that Devarddhi in the fifth or sixth century caused the Siddhānta to be written in books, and introduced the use of MSS. in the instruction of pupils and laymen. He takes only the latter statement to be true, and assumes that MSS. of the Aṅga and other sacred works did exist at an earlier period, 'because it is hardly credible that the Jaina monks should never before have attempted to write down what they had to commit to memory [1].'

There is only one important point on which Jacobi's answer is incomplete. It furnishes no instance in which the tradition of the Jaina is proved to be trustworthy by independent, really historical sources. This led Professor Bühler to enter on a careful re-examination of all the ancient historical documents which refer to the Jaina. The result has been that he has succeeded in proving the correctness of a great part of the larger list of teachers and schools, preserved in the Sthaviravāli of the Kalpa-Sūtra. The historical documents corroborating it are the well-known 'Muttra' Inscriptions, published in Sir A. Cunningham's *Archaeological Reports*, vol. iii. p. 31 ff., plates xiii–xv [2].

[1] S. B. E., vol. xxii., *Gaina-Sūtra*, pt. i. p. xxxviii.

[2] They not only mention the division of the Jaina monks into schools, lines of teachers, and branches, but contain the names of nine *gaṇa*, *kula*, and *śākha*, and of one teacher mentioned in the Kalpa-Sūtra.

These Inscriptions[1] bear the date of the era of Indo-Scythian kings over North-Western India, e.g. Kanishka, and though scholars are not quite agreed as to when to fix the beginning of this era, one of the latest dates assigned for Kanishka's accession to the throne is the year 78–79 A.D. The dialect in which they are written shows that curious mixture of Sanskrit and Prākrit which is found in the Gātha of the Northern Buddhists. From them we also learn that the Jaina monks of Mathurā formed, between 83 and 167 A.D., an order of a hierarchy, which was divided into several schools, each of which counted several subdivisions. Most of the persons named receive the title *vāchaka*, or preacher, which is still very commonly given to those ascetics who are considered fit to expound the sacred books to laymen and pupils. One, however, is styled *gaṇin*, 'chief of a school,' a somewhat higher title, which even to-day is conferred on an eminent Sādhu. Among the schools the *koṭikagaṇa* shows that it had had a long history, and may safely be considered as having been founded at least a century before the beginning of our era. The existence, therefore, of titles like *vāchaka* and *gaṇin*, and of ancient schools at the end of the first century A.D., shows that the Jaina sect had possessed already for a long time 'a continuous and self-conscious existence.' The Inscriptions further prove that the great schism which divided the Jaina into two hostile sections took place, not as modern tradition asserts (in 609 after Vīra), but long before the beginning of our era, thus confirming Jacobi's view already put forward. In this way the gap of ten centuries which exists between Vardhamāna and Devarddhi is almost filled up by continuous Jaina tradition. The two centuries during which alone no tradition is preserved are thought, by Jacobi, to have been filled up by the use of the fourteen Pūrva, of which more will be said later on.

[1] *Vienna Oriental Journal*, 1887, vol. i. pp. 169, 179–180.

The Age of Extant Jaina Literature.

The Jaina Canon, or Siddhānta, was drawn up at the council of Valabhi, under the presidency of Devarddhi. This date corresponds either to 454 or 467 A.D., and is incorporated into the Kalpa-Sūtra (§ 148). 'Devarddhi Gaṇin,' says the tradition, 'perceiving the Siddhānta in danger of becoming extinct, caused it to be written in books.' In olden times it had been the custom of the Brāhmans, and hence of the Buddhists and Jaina, to rely on the memory more than on MSS. How early these MSS. were first written we do not know, for no mention is made of them, but it is very likely that as soon as they settled in Upāśraya exclusively belonging to themselves, they began to keep them as they do now.

If this view be correct, Devarddhi 'arranged the already existing MSS. in a Canon, taking down from the mouth of learned theologians only such works as had not available MSS.' Then a great many copies were made, in order to furnish every seminary with books. In this way any single passage in a sacred text may have been introduced by the editor, and all we can say with certainty is that the bulk of the Siddhānta is not of his making.

What can be ascertained about the date of composition of the sacred books? There is no proof at all events that the first Tīrthakara was the revealer of their contents, though this is a dogmatic theory of the Jaina. But we have three methods by which to determine the latest date to which they may be assigned: the tests of scientific knowledge, of language, and of metres used. For instance, no traces of the elements of Greek astronomy can be found in the Siddhānta, and we know that these were introduced into India in the fourth century of our era. Evidently the Jaina Scriptures must have all been composed before then. The language too would give a perfect clue, if it were not that books may have been handed down, not in the language of composition, nor in that of pronunciation. Jacobi thinks that the language has been modernized, for the same word is not always spelt the same way in Jaina texts and MSS. It would be quite impossible, therefore, to restore Devarddhi's recension. But there are other differences between the original and present Siddhānta text. Weber speaks of 'lost passages which were extant at the date of the older commentaries, but also large interpolations which are apparent, and furthermore the text has even suffered complete transformations[1].' He attributes these changes, and the loss of the entire 'Dṛishṭivāda,' to the influence of the orthodox sect of Śvetāmbara, to whom the present Siddhānta exclusively belongs.

Probably we must regard these methods of spelling as historical; that is, all spellings were treated as authentic, and so were preserved. If this assumption is correct, the most archaic spelling represents pronunciation near the time of composition, while modern spelling dates back to the period shortly before the redaction of the Canon took place. Using this proposition, and comparing the Jaina Prākṛit in its oldest form with Pāli texts on the one side, and later Prākṛits on the other, we are led to the conclusion that the sacred books of the Jaina approximate more in point of time to the Southern Buddhists than to later Prākṛit writers.

An examination of the metres in use is a still safer guide. What do we find? It will be sufficient for the sake of example to take the Vaitālīya, Trishṭubh, and Āryā metres and discuss their use. We note then that the Jaina Sūtrakṛitāṅga-Sūtra has a whole lesson in the Vaitālīya metre; that Pāli verses of the Southern Buddhists and Sanskrit literature of the Northern Buddhists also use the metre;

[1] Weber's *Sacred Literature of the Jains*, translated by Dr. A. W. Smyth (1893), p. 8.

and further, that the Dhammapadam (of the Southern Buddhists) is written in an older style, whereas the Lalita Vistara (of the Northern Buddhists) is more modern in point of development. We conclude, therefore, that this one lesson in the Sūtrakṛitāṅga dates back to a period between the versifications of the Southern and Northern Buddhists.

Take the Āryā metre also as a confirmation of the above proof, and the Dhammapadam, which is composed in ancient Pāli, will be found to contain no such verses. Then notice that the Sūtrakṛitāṅga, just as we should expect if it is dated as we have suggested above, contains a whole lecture in an old form of Āryā; and the later the period the more common the Āryā metre, till it is found not only in the younger parts of the Siddhānta, and in Brāhman literature (whether in Prākṛit or Sanskrit), but also in the works of the Northern Buddhists (e.g. the Lalita Vistara).

Lastly, the form of the Trishṭubh metre in ancient Jaina works is younger than that in the Pāli literature and older than that in the Lalita Vistara. In all three cases then it appears that the Gātha of the Lalita Vistara are more modern than those in the Jaina Siddhānta. Hence Jacobi puts down 'the chronological position of the oldest parts of the Jaina literature as intermediate between the Pāli and the Lalita Vistara.'

We have seen that the date of the oldest works in the Jaina Canon makes them older than the Gātha of the Lalita Vistara. What date are we to assign to the latter? We know that it is said to have been translated into Chinese in 65 A.D. Therefore extant Jaina literature must all be placed earlier than our era. Again, from the close comparison of Pāli, Jaina, and later Prākṛits, it has been shown that Jaina literature resembles that of the Southern more than that of the Northern Buddhists. Compare this with Max Müller's conclusion to his discussion on the point, when he fixes the latest date of a Buddhist Canon at the time of the Second Council, 377 B.C., and it will be seen that *the whole of the Jaina Siddhānta was composed after the fourth century* B.C., *and before the Christian era.* It is interesting then to notice that the traditions of the Śvetāmbara agree fairly well with this independent reasoning. For they say that their Aṅga were brought together at the time when Kandragupta was on the throne. And this date is given by Max Müller as 315–291 B.C., and by Westergaard and Kern as 320 B.C. Therefore the composition of the Jaina Canon would fall somewhere between the end of the fourth and beginning of the third century B.C. Both sects of the Jaina attribute the collection of works to Bhadrabāhu.

Works older than the existing Canon.

Besides the Jaina Scriptures, the Śvetāmbara and Digambara speak of some older works called Pūrva, as well as the Aṅga. There were said to be fourteen of these, but in time the knowledge of them was lost, and they became totally extinct. The Śvetāmbara hold that these fourteen Pūrva were incorporated in the twelfth Aṅga, the Dṛishṭivāda, which was lost before the thousandth year of their era, i.e. before the redaction under Devarddhi. Anyhow a detailed account, or table of contents, is found in the fourth Aṅga, the Samavāyāṅga, and in the Nandī-Sūtra. There are two reasons for believing that this tradition is correct. First, the word 'pūrva' means 'former,' and second, the Aṅga do not derive their authority from the Pūrva, and there would be no need to fabricate the idea.

How then was it that the Pūrva were superseded by a new Canon? Weber thinks that the Śvetāmbara lost the Dṛishṭivāda, because they had begun so to differ from the tenets of the book that the Pūrva fell into neglect[1]. Jacobi holds that the Pūrva were probably only of temporary value, and contained accounts of philosophical controversies held between Mahāvīra and his rivals. The title 'pravada' which is added to the name of every Pūrva seems to favour this view. Whereas if the Śvetāmbara be accused of losing the Pūrva, the Digambara seem to have lost their Aṅga as well within the first two centuries after the Nirvāṇa.

In this case the neglect of the Pūrva was due, not so much to any direct intention, as to the fact that the new Canon set forth the Jaina doctrines in a clearer light.

Contents of the Siddhānta.

What then was the Canon of the Jaina Scriptures which Devarddhi Gaṇin compiled? The Siddhānta, as we now have it, is divided into forty-five Āgama, in six groups; several of the texts of the Āgama having distinct names as authors. There are:—

I. Eleven Aṅga.
II. Twelve Upāṅga.
III. Ten Païnna.
IV. Six Chēda.
V. Two Sūtra (Nandī and Anuyōgadvāra).
VI. Four Mūla-Sūtra.

Weber has shown that 'the oldest portions of their literature are in reality nothing but *disjecta membra*; that they are very unequal, and, as regards the date of their composition, separated from each other by extensive periods.' Yet he admits that 'a hand, aiming at unification and order, has been brought to bear especially upon the *aṅga* and *upāṅga*.' Jacobi also considers that the redaction of the *aṅga* took place early, and tradition places the event under Bhadrabāhu.

[1] *Indische Studien*, xvi. p. 248.

III.

The Antiquity of Jaina Philosophy.

When we come to consider how old Jaina doctrines are, and compare them with that of other schools of thought in India, we find that Jaina ethics are generally based on primitive ideas. As illustrations of these notions, nearly everything is possessed of a soul; not only have plants their own souls, but particles of earth, cold water, fire, and wind also[1].

Now ethnology teaches us that animism is the basis of many beliefs that have been called 'the philosophy of savages'; and that when civilization advances, some kind of anthropomorphism takes its place. Therefore it is natural to conclude that animistic beliefs must have been fairly prevalent, in large classes of Indian society, when Jainism first took its rise. And since this must have happened at an early date, it points to the antiquity of Jaina philosophy[2].

Another mark Jainism has in common with the oldest Brāhman philosophies, Vēdānta and Sāṅkhya. The category of Quality is not yet clearly and distinctly conceived, but is just evolving out of the category of Substance. That is to say, things which we recognize as qualities are constantly mistaken for and mixed up with substances. For instance, the Sūtra rarely use the expression 'guṇa,' or 'qualities'; but more modern books regularly do so, showing the idea to be a later innovation. Again, the terms 'dharma' and 'adharma' (merit and demerit) are treated of as kinds of substances with which the soul comes in contact. Now Professor Oldenberg has pointed out that this was distinctly a primitive conception of the Vedic Hindū, and such a confusion of ideas would never have occurred at a later period.

[1] S. B. E., vol. xlv. p. xxxii.
[2] Ibid., p. xxxiii.

Some Early Jaina Doctrines.

Have we any means of discovering what was the teaching of early days, and whether it corresponded with the doctrines of Mahāvīra? It will be admitted, from what has been said above, that the Nigaṇṭha or Nirgrantha, now better known as Jaina or Arhata, already existed as an important sect when the Buddhist church was being founded. In order, therefore, to come to a solution of the above question, perhaps it will be best to take from published Buddhist and Jaina works, as the oldest witnesses that we can summon, available information about the Nigaṇṭha, their doctrines and religious practices [1].

I. *The Eternity of Ātman.*

There were at the time of the Buddhists and Jaina several other schools of philosophy, whom they each called heretics. And it will not be out of place to mention what were their theories about Ātman, the 'soul,' or as Professor Max Müller prefers to translate it—'the self.' First, there were three materialist schools—the one contending that the body and the soul are one and the same; the second, that the five elements are eternal and constitute everything, as in the following lines:—

'Man (purusho) consists of four elements; when he dies, earth returns to earth, water to water, fire to fire, wind to wind, and the organs of sense merge into air' (or space—'*Ākāsa*') [1];

the third school was a variety of the second, and is thus described:—

'Some say that there are five elements and the soul is sixth (substance), but they contend that the soul and the world (i. e. the five elements) are eternal. "These (six substances) do not perish neither (without nor with a cause); the non-existent does not come into existence, but all things are eternal by their very nature [2]."'

[1] Cf. S. B. E., vol. xlv., *Sūtrakṛitāṅga*, ii. 1, 20-23.
[2] S. B. E., ibid., i. 1, 15, 16.

Then we find a fourth school of Fatalists described as saying:—

'But misery (and pleasure) is not caused by (the souls) themselves; how could it be caused by other (agents, as time, &c.)? Pleasure and misery, final beatitude and temporal (pleasure and pain) are not caused by (the souls) themselves, nor by others; but the individual souls experience them; it is the lot assigned them by destiny[1].'

Lastly, four schools of Agnostics are given us—Kriyāvāda, Akriyāvāda, Agṅānavāda, and Vaṁayikavāda. All these were considered by the Jaina as heretical. These Agnostics, or Agṅānika, negatived all modes of expression of the existence or non-existence of a thing, if it were anything transcendental or beyond human experience. And yet there is little doubt that Mahāvīra owed some of his conceptions to these very heretics, and formulated others under the influences of the day[2]. For instance, the doctrine of Syādvāda is identically the same as the Saptabhaṅgīnaya of the Jaina. It was an ingenious way out of the maze of the Agṅānavāda assertions about existence and non-existence.

Amidst all these conflicting views of the Soul, Mahāvīra kept to the old Brāhman idea of the Atman. He held that it was eternal, but that the Ātman have only a limited space, instead of being co-extensive with the universe.

II. *The Kriyāvāda*, or the doctrine which teaches that 'the soul acts or is affected by acts.'

There is a story told of Sīha, the general, a lay disciple of Nātaputta, in the sixth Khandhaka of the Mahāvagga. He wanted to pay Buddha a visit, and went to ask Nātaputta's leave. This was Nātaputta's answer:—

'Why should you, Sīha, who believe in the result of actions (according to their moral merit), go to visit the Samaṇa Gautama, who denies the result of actions? He teaches the doctrine of non-action; and in this doctrine he trains his disciples.'

[1] S. B. E., *Sūtrakṛitāṅga*, i. 1, 2, 2, 3.

[2] Cf. what Mahāvīra taught about the Kriyāvāda himself lower down.

This doctrine of Kriyāvāda was opposed by Buddha's bold teaching about Akriyāvāda, which said that 'the soul does not exist, or that it does not act, or is not affected by acts.' Here we recognize the teaching of the different schools of materialists, and in the Brāhman philosophy of the Vedānta, Sāṅkhya, and Yōga schools of thought. Mahāvīra, on the other hand, agreed with the Vaiśeshika and Nyāya schools of Brāhman philosophy.

III. *Annihilation of Karman.*

The teaching of Nigaṇṭha Nātaputta on this point is thus described by Abhaya, a learned Buddhist:—

> 'He teaches the annihilation (by austerities) of the old Karman, and the prevention (by inactivity) of new Karman. When Karman ceases, misery ceases; when misery ceases, perception ceases; when perception ceases, every misery will come to an end. In this way a man is saved by pure annihilation of sin (niġġara), which is really effective [1].'

Very similar is the doctrine of the later books of the Siddhānta.

> 'By austerities he cuts off Karman [2].'
>
> 'By renouncing activity he obtains inactivity: by ceasing to act he acquires no new Karman, and destroys the Karman he had acquired before [2].'
>
> 'Karman is the root of birth and death, and birth and death they call misery [2].'
>
> 'A man who is indifferent to the object of the senses, and to the other feelings of the mind, is free from sorrows; though still in the Saṃsāra, he is not afflicted by that long succession of pains, just as the leaf of the Lotus (is not moistened) by water [3].'

IV. *The three Daṇḍa* (*daṇḍa* being a word meaning 'punishment'). Nigaṇṭha Upāli, who like Sīha was converted to Buddha's teaching, tells us that there are three daṇḍa, the daṇḍa of the body, that of the speech, and that of the mind. This is almost identical with the Jaina doctrine. For we are told that Nātaputta 'also declared that there were three daṇḍa or agents for the commission of sin, and that the acts of the

[1] *Aṅguttara Nikāya*, iii. 74.

[2] S. B. E., vol. xlv. p. xv., and *Uttarādhyayana*, Lect. xxix. §§ 27, 37, 71, 72.

[3] Ibid., xxxii. vv. 7, 34, 47, &c.

body (kāya), of the speech (vāch), and of the mind (mana), were three separate causes, each acting independently of the other[1].' He adds that the Nigaṇṭha considered sins of the body more important than sins of the mind, and that this was a point of contention between Jaina and Buddhists. We have a direct confirmation of this fact in Jaina works, for the very question as to whether sin may be committed unconsciously is discussed there, and a bold affirmative is given[2]. But lower down the Buddhists are even ridiculed for maintaining that the intention of a man decides whether a deed be sin or not[3].

V. *Pārśva and the doctrine of 'ḳātuyāma saṃvarasamvutō.'* This word, translated 'restraint in four directions[4],' is equivalent to the Prākṛit kātuggāma, a well-known Jaina term which denotes the '*four vows of Pārśva*' in contradistinction to the five vows of Mahāvīra. Here the Buddhists have *probably* made a mistake in ascribing to Mahāvīra a doctrine which properly belonged to his predecessor Pārśva. Professor Jacobi, therefore, looks upon this as a proof that the Jaina tradition is correct, in asserting that 'followers of Pārśva actually existed at the time of Mahāvīra.'

Pārśva's followers are mentioned in the Jaina Sūtra in quite a matter-of-fact way (especially Kēśi, who seems to have been a leader of the sect in the time of Mahāvīra), so that there is no reason to doubt the authenticity of these records. There is an interesting legend of how the old and new body were united[5]. And indications of some estrangement, even then, though not open hostility, may point to the cause of the division of the body into Śvetāmbara

[1] *Indian Antiquary*, vol. ix. p. 159.

[2] S. B. E., vol. xlv., *Sūtrakṛitāṅga*, ii. 4, p. 399.

[3] Ibid., ii. 6, pp. 414–416.

[4] Cf. *Indian Antiquary*, ix. 158 ff., 'On Mahāvīra and his predecessors.'

[5] Cf. *Uttarādhyayana*, Lect. xxiii.

and Digambara. It was evidently a matter of time, and in the end developed into a great schism.

Also the *Nigaṇṭha* are frequently mentioned in the Piṭaka, as opponents or converts of Buddha and his disciples. They must have been an important sect by the time Buddhism took its rise. Hence they must have existed before Nātaputta.

There is yet another proof. Makkhali Gōsāla divided mankind into six classes, and the third were the Nigaṇṭha. Hence, since he was a contemporary of Buddha and Mahāvīra, it is clear that the Nigaṇṭha had already attained to great importance.

Early Religious Practices.

Jacobi has deciphered some exhortations to a Sāvaka, or Nigaṇṭha layman, as follows[1]:—

> 'Well, sir, you must desist from doing injury to beings in the East beyond a yōgana from here, or to those in the West, North, South, always beyond a yōgana from here[2].'

This is evidently a trace of *the Digvirati vow* of the Jaina, which lays down limits beyond which one shall not travel or do business in different directions.

Again, later on it says:—

> 'Well, sir, take off all your clothes and declare:—I belong to nobody, and nobody belongs to me.'

According to this statement, the *duties of a Nigaṇṭha layman* became during certain days equal to those of a monk; it was on common days only that the difference between a layman and monk was realized.

Comparing this rule with that of present-day observances of the Jaina, throughout these specified days, we seem to see that Jaina have abated somewhat in their rigidity with regard to the duties of a layman.

[1] *Aṅguttara Nikāya*, iii. 70, 3.

[2] Pali Text Society, *Sumaṅgala Vilāsinī*, p. 119.

Also Buddhaghōsa says that the Nigaṇṭha hold the opinion that '*the soul has no colour*,' in contradistinction to the Āgīvika, who divide mankind into six classes according to the colour of the soul (Ātman). Both Nigaṇṭha and Āgīvika, however, agree that '*the soul continues to exist after death* and is free from ailments' (arōgō).

Again, Buddhaghōsa says that Nigaṇṭha Nātaputta considers *cold water* to be *possessed of life*, for which reason he does not use it. This is of course a well-known doctrine of the Jaina.

Leading Jaina Doctrines of To-day.

We do not intend to discuss all the present-day doctrines of the Jaina, which constitute the philosophy of their system, but only a few of the leading tenets. According to original authorities, all objects—sensible or abstract—are arranged under nine categories, termed Tattva (truths or existences).

I. Jiva, or 'life,' is reducible to two classes. The first comprises animals, men, demons, and gods; the second, all combinations of the four elements—earth, water, fire, air—and all the products of the vegetable kingdom. These are further arranged into five classes, according to the number of *Indriya* they possess. It is a peculiarity of the Jaina notions of life, that it is always adapted to the body it animates, diminishing with the gnat and expanding with the elephant. Life is defined, generically, as having no beginning or ending, but endowed with its own attributes of agent and enjoyer, proportionate to the body it animates. Through sin it passes into animals, through virtue and vice combined it passes into men, through virtue alone it ascends to heaven; through the annihilation of both vice and virtue it obtains emancipation.

II. Ajīva, or 'inertia,' comprises objects or properties devoid of consciousness and life. These are vaguely classed, and generally incapable of interpretation. Their number is commonly set down as fourteen, the symbol of vitality. For Ajīva, as well as Jiva, can never be destroyed, though its form may change.

III. Puṇya, or 'good,' is whatever causes happiness to living beings. There are as many as forty-two kinds of goodness enumerated.

IV. Pāpa, or 'ill,' is the cause of man's unhappiness; eighty-two kinds are enumerated.

V. Āsrava is the source from which the evil acts of living beings proceed. There are five specified sources—the Indriya or organs of sense, the Kashāya or passions, the Avrata or non-observance of positive commands, and the Yōga or attachment of the mind, speech, and body to any act; and last of all, the Kriyā or acts, which are prompted in twenty-six different ways.

VI. Saṃvara is the cause by which acts are stored up or impeded. The ingenious Jaina can think of fifty-seven ways in which this can be done, e. g. by secrecy, endurance, gentleness.

VII. Nirjarā is the religious practice that destroys mortal impurities. It is a kind of penance, positive because repentant, and negative because of fasting and continence.

VIII. Bandha is the association of life with acts, as of milk with water, or fire with a red-hot iron.

IX. Moksha is the last of the nine principles, and consists in the liberation of the spirit from the bonds of action. It amounts to exemption from the incidents of life, and from the necessity of being born again. It implies profound calm, as of a fire gone out, or of the setting of a star, or of the dying of a saint. 'It is not annihilation but increasing apathy which they (both Jaina and Buddhists) understand to be the extinction of their saints, and which they esteem to be supreme felicity.'

The means by which *moksha* is to be attained are called, as in the case of Buddhism, the three jewels—right faith, right knowledge, and right conduct. Right faith is unswerving belief in the Jīna, who was originally a man 'bound,' like others, but who has attained by his own exertions to emancipation and complete knowledge, and has preached the truth to suffering humanity.

Right knowledge is the knowledge of the system promulgated by the Jīna:—'The world of Brāhman cosmology is uncreated and eternal. Its component parts are six substances, Souls, Dharma (or moral merit), Adharma (or sin), space, time, and atoms of matter. By the combination of these atoms are produced the four elements, and human bodies, as well as the phenomena of the world of sense, and the heavenly worlds. The Jaina are as extravagant with regard to time as with regard to space. They consider that human bodies and human lives increase during the Utsarpiṇī, and diminish during the Avasarpiṇī—periods of incredible length. The doctrine of bondage of souls, as held by the Jaina, is practically identical with the views held by Indian thinkers generally. But they stand alone in maintaining that souls are to be found 'in apparently lifeless masses, in stone, in clods of earth, in drops of water, in fire, and in wind.'

Right conduct divides itself into two branches, according as it is incumbent upon the Jaina monk or layman. The Jaina monk, as we have seen above, on entering the order takes five vows; not only is he to abstain from these sins himself in thought, word, and deed, but he is not to cause others to be guilty of them. These rules are carried out to the letter. The rules binding on laymen are less strict. They are expected to abstain from gross violation of the five precepts. They must be faithful to the marriage vow, and promise not to increase their wealth by unfair means. It is all the more remarkable, therefore, that Jaina laymen are noted for their wealth. They are of course forbidden to indulge in flesh and spirituous drinks, and any other kinds of food (e.g. honey) which involve injury to animal life. Agriculture too is forbidden, as an injury to the 'earth-body.' Even the ordering another man to plough a field is stigmatized as a sin.

The result of all this teaching has been to make Jaina laymen serious, well-conducted, and humane men, ready to endure great sacrifices for their religion, and especially for the welfare of animals. Advantage has been taken of this, under British rule, to enlist their sympathies with veterinary science[1].

Jaina Ritual and Pantheon.

Bühler thinks that the original atheistic system of the Jaina was fitted out with an elaborate cult, as a concession to the lay mind. It is anyhow evident from the 'Kathākoça,' or Jaina folk-lore, that the Jaina worship many gods. Their chief objects of worship are the Jīna, or Tīrthakara, whom they adore with flowers and incense and candles. Hymns of praise are sung in their honour, and pilgrimages are made to places hallowed by their memories. But, like the Buddhists, they allow the existence of the Hindū gods, and have admitted into their worship any of those that are connected with the tales of their saints, e.g. Indra, Śakra, Garuḍa, Sarasvatī, Lakshmī. They have quite a pantheon, now, of Bhuvanapati, Asura, Nāga, Gandhana, &c., inhabiting the celestial and infernal regions, mountains, forests, and lower air[2].

Each Tīrthakara has a separate *chiṅha*, or sign, which is usually placed below his image. An excellent list of the Jīna, from Ṛishabha to Mahāvīra, appears in Burgess's *Cave Temples of India*[2]. Each Jīna is

[1] Tawney, *Kathākoça*, pp. xii–xv. (Oriental Translation Fund. New Series, ii. 1895.)

[2] Fergusson and Burgess, *Cave Temples of India*, p. 488.

accompanied by his distinctive sign (e.g. vṛisha, bull, śesha, hooded snake), his colour, and his place of Nirvāṇa. There are five favourites among the twenty-four, especially the first, twenty-third, and twenty-fourth.

Jaina Temples.

The Jaina possess some of the most remarkable places of pilgrimage in India, situated in the midst of most lovely mountain scenery, in the west, and south, and east. At *Palitana*, in Kathiawar, West India, is the temple-covered hill of Satrunjaya, the most sacred of the pilgrimage-resorts of the Jaina, so that Jaina from all parts of India desire to erect temples upon it. There are temples of every size, from three feet square to large marble halls, with columns and towers and plenty of openings. The latter are thus graphically described by Fergusson[1]:—'They are situated in *tuks*, or separate enclosures, surrounded by high fortified walls; the smaller ones line the silent streets. A few *yati*, or priests, sleep in the temples, and perform the daily services, and a few attendants are constantly there to keep the place clean, or to feed the sacred pigeons, who are the sole denizens of the spot; but there are no human habitations, properly so called, within the walls. The pilgrim or the stranger ascends in the morning, and returns when he has performed his devotions or satisfied his curiosity. He must not eat, or at least must not cook his food, on the sacred hill, and he must not sleep there. It is the city of the gods, and meant for them only, and not intended for the use of mortals.' Some of these temples date from the eleventh century, but the majority have been built in the present century.

The other most important place of pilgrimage in the west was Mount Abu, on the borders of Rajpu-

[1] Fergusson, *History of Architecture*, vol. iii. bk. ii. p. 226.

tāna. Five temples, wholly of white marble, are built there, which for minute delicacy of carving and beauty stand almost unrivalled. It is a beautiful spot, 'rising from the desert as abruptly as an island from the ocean,' and presenting on almost every side inaccessible scarps 5,000 ft. or 6,000 ft. high. 'The summit can only be approached by ravines that cut into its sides.' This makes it all the more remarkable that the white marble should have been conveyed there, for no quarries are to be found within three hundred miles of the spot, and the carrying work must have involved immense expense.

The highest point of the Bengal range of hills was also selected by the Jaina as a sacred spot. 'No less than nineteen of their twenty-four Tīrthakara are said to have died and been buried there, among others Parasnath, the last but one, and he consequently gave the hill the name it now bears. . . . Before, however, Jainism became politically important, the centre of power had gravitated towards the west. Were it not for this, there seems little doubt but that Parasnath would have been more important in their eyes than Palitana and Girnar[1].'

Other temples in North Jaina style are found at Girnar, Gwalior, and Khajurāho; but in Southern India they are divided into two classes, called Bastī and Bettu. The former are temples containing an image of one of the twenty-four Tīrthakara; but the latter are not temples in the ordinary sense of the word, but courtyards open to the sky, containing images, not of a Tīrthakara, but of one Gōmati, who is unknown to the Northern Jaina. These kinds of temples are found at Sravana Belgula, Moodbidri, and Gurusaukerry[2].

[1] Fergusson, *History of Architecture*, vol. iii. bk. ii. pp. 240, 241.
[2] Ibid., p. 265 ff.

CHAPTER III

THE SĪKH

'The Name of Jesus Christ . . . Neither is there any other Name under heaven, that is given among men, wherein we must be saved.'—Acts iv. 10, 12 (R.V.).

I. Circumstances under which Sīkhism came into existence—The era of modern Hindūism—The Vaishṇava—Kabīr.

II. The history of the Sīkh—Religious and political—The ten Gurū—Gōvind Singh and the Khālsā—Sīkh wars—British occupation of the Panjāb.

III. The Granth or sacred book of the Sīkh—Its two parts—Its language and authors—Cardinal doctrines—The Unity of the Supreme Being—Relation of man to the Supreme—The origin of sin—Life after death—The means of emancipation—The authority of the Gurū.

IV. Other Sīkh observances—The golden temple at Amritsar—Sīkh population and denominations—Christian missions to the Panjāb.

The Era of Modern Hindūism.

THE period of the Reformation in Europe was also a time of religious movements in India. The final triumph of ancient Brāhmanism over modern Buddhism in India had taken place, after a struggle in which the former was profoundly influenced by the latter. And modern Hindūism had arisen as the third and most complex phase of Hindū religious thought. The victory was gained at the cost of many changes, of an endless number of sects which arose, 'each exalting its own god to the place of supreme.' The popular craving for personal objects of faith and devotion had to be satisfied by subordinating the purely spiritual Brahm, with its first manifestation Brahmā, to the personal deities Śiva and Vishṇu or to some form of these deities [1].

[1] Monier-Williams, *Religious Life and Thought in India*, p. 54.

This chapter is to be devoted to the consideration of one of the most interesting of these modern sects, interesting because it gave birth to a nation. A few words of introduction are felt to be necessary.

There are three principal classes of the present-day Hindū, namely, (1) Smārta, (2) Ṡaiva, (3) Vaishṇava; and each has a distinctive school of thought attached to it.

'The first class believes that man's spirit is identical with the one infinite Spirit (Ātmā, Brahmă), which is the substratum of the Universe and only cognizable through internal meditation and self-communion. They are also believers in the Tri-mūrti; that is, in the three personal gods, Brahmā, Vishṇu, and Ṡiva—with their train of subordinate deities—but only as co-equal manifestations of the one eternal, impersonal Spirit, and as destined ultimately to be re-absorbed into that Spirit, and so disappear.' These are the orthodox followers of Ṡaṅkara[1].

'The second class of Hindū consists of the Ṡaiva, who are believers in one god Ṡiva, the one supreme personal God, the one Self-existent Being, identified with the one Spirit of the Universe, and therefore not liable to lose his personality by reabsorption into that Spirit.'

'The third class consists of the Vaishṇava, who are believers in one personal god Vishṇu, above every other god, including Ṡiva. This one god exists in an eternal body, which is antecedent to his earthly incarnations and survives all his incarnations[1].'

The Vaishṇava.

It is with one sect of the Vaishṇava that we have to deal in this chapter. Let us first, however, glance at the character of Vaishṇavism itself. At the outset we see that it is a form of monotheism, and presents the essential elements of a genuine religion, namely,

[1] Monier-Williams, *Religious Life and Thought in India*, p. 95 ff.

a personal devotion to a personal God, by trusting him, loving him, praying to him, and obeying him. Vishṇu is represented as a god that evinced sympathy with mundane suffering, was interested in human affairs, and active for the welfare of all created things. This caused his frequent descents (avatāra) on earth under various forms. Such a god was needed for India, and hence arose teachers, among whom was Śāṇḍilya, who insisted upon the doctrine of salvation by love and devotion (bhakti), a doctrine which was fully propounded in the Bhagavad-gītā and Bhāgavata-purāṇa. We cannot wonder that devotion to Vishṇu in his two incarnations, Rāma and Kṛishṇa, became the most popular religion of India. Nor is it difficult to understand that the condition of Vaishṇavism depends largely upon personal leadership and influence, and is one of perpetual decay and revival, collapse and recovery.

Kabīr.

Among the more important of the minor sects of Vaishṇavism was that founded by Rāmānanda early in the fourteenth century. The sect of Kabīr (Kabīr Panthī) is always included among the Vaishṇava sects, because the founder was reputed to have been a disciple of Rāmānanda. Kabīr's teaching undoubtedly had much influence throughout Upper India in the fifteenth and sixteenth centuries. And his sayings are constantly quoted by Gurū Nānak and his successors, who were the authors of the sacred writings of the Granth. It is clear that his teaching exerted considerable influence over the Sīkh religion. In these teachings of his, Kabīr sets himself against the whole body of Hindū superstitions, ridiculing the Shāstra and Purāṇa, rejecting every distinction of caste, religion, and sect, and condemning idolatry and everything approaching to it[1].

[1] Monier-Williams, *Religious Life and Thought in India*, pp. 158–160.

His positive doctrines and precepts are embodied in numerous collections in Hindī, as well as in the Sīkh 'Granth.' From these we gather that the keynote of his teaching was submission, in matters of faith and morals, to the authority of the *Gurū*[1]. Not that he ever claimed infallibility for his own utterances, for he constantly warned his disciples to investigate for themselves the truth of every word he uttered.

If this man was the most perfect representative of a reforming movement, it is unfortunate that so little is known of his antecedents. The Mohammedans claim him as one of themselves, and among the Hindū there is a widespread tradition which represents him as having been converted from Mohammedanism. And there is no doubt that the teaching of the Vedānta, as expounded by him, found its way into the Granth through the respect paid by the Gurū to his life.

The History of the Sīkh.

With the above introduction, it is time to turn to the history of the Sīkh religion itself. It will be well to divide the history into two parts :—

(*a*) The Religious History. (*b*) The Political History.

(*a*) THE RELIGIOUS HISTORY begins with Gurū Bābā Nānak Bedī, who is known to have been born in 1469, not far from Lahore in the Panjāb. His biographies in Panjābi are filled with myths and stories of miraculous events connected with him, invented soon after his death. But there is no reason to doubt that at an early age he associated himself with religious leaders of all kinds, and wandered to various shrines 'in search of some clue to the labyrinth of Hindūism.' It is even affirmed that he went to Mecca. He laid no claim, however, to be the originator of a new religion, but mainly founded his teaching on

[1] Barth, *The Religions of India*, pp. 239, 240.

that of his predecessors, especially that of Kabīr, whom he constantly quoted. It does not appear that Nānak directly attacked or denounced caste, as Kabīr did, but rather tolerated it as a civil institution, and aimed at delivering Hindūism, and especially the Vaishṇavism of Northern India, from superstition and idolatry. Thus he rejected the Veda, the Shāstra, and the Purāṇa, as well as the Koran, and yet the Brāhman was to be treated with respect. 'There are neither Hindū nor Musalmans' was the subject, we are told, of one of his first sermons.

Nānak's death, we know, occurred on October 10, 1538. One of his sons was expected to succeed him, but to the surprise of those present at his death-bed he nominated, as second *Gurū*, his devoted disciple Lahanā, of Trehan clan. His devotion to his master seems to have been his chief merit, for he was quite illiterate. He appointed Bābā Amar-Dās Bhallā to succeed him.

For nearly a century the Sīkh appear to have remained a purely religious community of inoffensive Puritans. As far as the fifth *Gurū*, the supreme authority was transmitted by means of consecration, at the hands of the dying teacher, to the worthiest of his disciples[1]. The name Sīkh means 'disciple,' and the strength of the movement lay in the relation of the disciple to the 'Gurū[2]' or spiritual guide. All this time the Mogul dynasty had been rising under Babar and his successor Humayun, till under the long reign of Akbar (1556–1605) the Sīkh increased greatly in number and power. This more than tolerant Mohammedan emperor sought diligently for a knowledge of other faiths, and Amar-Dās, the third Gurū, was one of those who had conference with him. His successor and son-in-law, Gurū Bābā Rām-Dās

[1] Barth, *The Religions of India*, p. 245.

[2] 'By the term Gurū, the Sīkhs mean a person who stands between them and their God, and who has full control over their spiritual welfare.'—*Sadler*.

Soḍhī, received from Akbar a gift of a piece of land, on which he dug the large square tank afterwards called Amritsar [1] ('the pool of immortality'). It was in the last year of this Gurū's life that several Jesuit fathers from Goa were invited by Akbar to visit the Panjāb. It is important to notice that, from the time of Rām-Dās Soḍhī, the fourth *Gurū*, the succession became hereditary (1581). An authentic story tells us that this was granted by the third Gurū to his daughter on account of her devotion to her father. She asked for and was granted by him the three following requests:—(1) That her husband should succeed her father, (2) that the succession should become hereditary, (3) that the Soḍhī should be respected sixteen times more than the descendants of any former Gurū. The remaining five Gurū were regarded as rulers, rather than as teachers. Arjan's works are manifold. He compiled the sacred book called the *Ādi Granth*, the materials for which he had received unarranged from his father. Thus he provided the Sīkh with a written standard of authority. He built the Golden Temple in the middle of his father's tank, and thus formed the nucleus of the sacred town Amritsar, which is still the metropolis and holy place of the Sīkh religion. He established a regular system of tax-collecting from all adherents to the sect in different places. It is not surprising then to learn that his power and prosperity only lasted during Akbar's lifetime, or that he incurred the displeasure of Jahāngīr, Akbar's successor, and was imprisoned (1606), and died soon after; for the Mohammedan government could scarcely permit of the growth of an *imperium in imperio*.

From this moment the community of the Sīkh rapidly changes into a military theocracy, to which the fierce population of the Jāts supplied a fanatical soldiery. The promulgation of the Granth for the instruction of the people had made a way for this

[1] Sir William Hunter, *Indian Empire*, p. 808.

change in the character of the leadership. The work of the teacher was now in great measure transferred to the guardians of the sacred volume, who read it in the ears of the people. The lives of Gurū Har-Gōvind, Gurū Har-Raī, and Gurū Har-Kishau are comparatively unimportant. But the ninth *Gurū*, Tēg-Bahādur, attracted the attention of the fanatical Emperor Aurangzīb. Whether it was the emperor's fanaticism, or the fault of this contemplative Gurū, he was put to death, without cause, at Delhi (1675). This roused the Sīkh to greater zeal, and henceforward they became a nation of fighting-men.

(*b*) Political History. Gurū Gōvind Raī Soḍhī, son of Tēg-Bahādur, after passing some years in retirement and study, came forth a vigorous and enthusiastic leader with high aims. If Gurū Nānak was the founder of the Sīkh religion, Gurū Gōvind would be the founder of the Sīkh nationality. He therefore set himself the task of organizing the Sīkh of the Panjāb, who were now becoming formidable for their number, their physique, and their warlike propensities. The first adherents of Nānak had been mostly Jāts or Khattris. Many of them were men of great stature and powerful frame. As Sīkh they acquired a distinctive appearance, by giving up the Hindū practice of shaving the head and face. They were forbidden the use of tobacco.

All Gōvind's plans were directed towards increasing the distinction between his followers and Hindū and Mohammedans in general. First he called the sect by the name of 'Khālsā,' borrowed from the Arabic 'Khalas,' meaning 'pure.' Then he surrounded it with a number of regulations, under the influence of which it became a people by itself, devoted to triumph or extermination. All social inequality was abolished in the heart of the Khālsā body, every member of which received the aristocratic surname of Singh (in Sanskrit *singha*, lion), and this at the risk of offending the most inveterate Hindū prejudices.

Costume was regulated in a uniform fashion, and every disciple was bound to have with him five marks of his discipleship, each beginning with the letter Kakka (K), viz. *long hair, a comb, a two-edged knife, a bangle, and breeches reaching to the knee.* With the exception of the religious respect paid to cows, all usages, practices, and ceremonies of Hindūism were rigorously prescribed; although Bābā Gōvind Singh Soḍhī himself personally took a part in one of the worst Hindū superstitions, to the extent of sacrificing one of his followers to propitiate the goddess Durgā. There was henceforth to be a distinct rite of initiation, known as the Pauhal and consisting of a kind of sherbet. Sugar is mixed with water by means of a two-edged knife, while the *Gurū* reads the first part of the Jăpjī. This mixture is then dashed on the head, face, and eyes, and sprinkled over other parts of the body of each new disciple, and the rest is given him to drink. From the moment of initiation the Sīkh became a soldier, and the holy war his permanent occupation. He was not even to return a salute from a Hindū. Besides these rites, iron came henceforth to be respected, and thereby certain superstitious practices crept into this iconoclastic religion. The Sīkh soldier prays before handling his sword; and the book of the Granth has become an object of adoration. Lastly, Gōvind tried to procure the original book of the Ādi Granth, as drawn up by Gurū Arjan, in order to introduce into it a more martial spirit. He was, however, foiled in this by the other Soḍhī, to whom the volume had been entrusted, as they did not acknowledge Gōvind as *Gurū*. The cumbersome supplement that he composed was then called 'The Granth of the Tenth Reign.'

The object of his life Gōvind could not indeed carry out, for it was an unequal struggle against the formidable empire of Aurangzīb. After thirty years of fighting, what remained of his faithful ones were dispersed among the mountains, while he accepted a post of command in the imperial armies, and fell at last by the hand of an Afghan assassin near Nander in the territories of the Nizam [1]. The Sīkh had not adopted all his reforms, and he appears to have clearly foreseen that at the stage which the sect had reached, the personal influence of the *Gurū* would henceforth be a source of schism, rather than of union. Therefore when pressed on his death-bed to appoint his successor, he declared that the dignity was abolished, and that the Granth would for the future be the *Gurū* of the Sīkhs.

After his decease the direction of the Khālsā body is said by some to have passed into the hands of an ascetic named Bāndā, who introduced further novelties of usage, such as the prohibition of spirituous liquors (in addition to that of tobacco). This only caused divisions, and infuriated resistance. Besides all this, the forces of the Khālsā were again and again massacred and nearly annihilated by the generals of the Emperor Farokhsir. Therefore after Bāndā's death by torture (1716) the direction of the sect fell into the hands of a military corporation of zealots, the Ākāli, 'The Faithful of the Eternal,' instituted, they say, by Gurū Gōvind himself. When the dissolution of the Mogul empire permitted the Sīkh to regain a footing on the plain, the Ākāli set themselves up as the guardians of the sanctuary of Amritsar, where the original copy of the Granth of Gurū Arjan was preserved. On great occasions they summoned together here the *Gurmatā*, or 'the Council of the Gurū,' the general assembly of the Sīkh chiefs, in which the supreme, temporal, and spiritual authority of the nation was vested, and which kept up in the sect a sufficient coherence and prevented the occurrence of new divisions in the bosom of the Khālsā [2].

[1] Elphinstone, *History of India*, book xii. p. 679 (1866 edition).
[2] Barth, *The Religions of India*, p. 248.

The rest of the history is entirely political, and can be soon told. First, the Sīkh recovered to their federation the greater part of the Jāt Sirdārs, who had carved out for themselves small feudal states on either side of the Sutlej. In 1764, after the final retreat of the Afghans, they took possession of Lahore, and became undisputed masters of the Panjāb; they could at that time muster 70,000 cavalry. Then arose Ranjīt Singh, 'the Lion of the Panjāb' (1797–1839), who (having obtained the appointment of Governor of Lahore from the Afghan Amīr) proved to be the consolidator of the power of the Sīkh, and soon made himself master of the whole Panjāb. He set himself the task of basing a personal despotism upon the religious fanaticism of the Sīkh. The British, whose power in India was rapidly extending, were at this time desirous of an alliance with Lahore. A British envoy, Mr. Charles Metcalfe, was received by Ranjīt at Kasūr in 1809, and an alliance was formed. The Khālsā were organized into an army, under European officers, which for steadiness and religious fervour has had no parallel since the 'Ironsides' of Cromwell. Till his death in 1839 Ranjīt Singh was ever loyal to the engagements he had entered into with Metcalfe in 1809. But he left no son capable of wielding his sceptre, and Lahore was torn by dissensions. The only strong power was the army of the Khālsā, which, after the disastrous defeat of the British arms in Afghanistan in 1842, burned to measure its strength with the British sepoys. The French generals, Avitabile and Court, were foolishly ousted, and the supreme military command was vested in a series of *panchāyats*, or elective committees of five.

In 1845, then, the Sīkh army, numbering 60,000 men with 150 guns, crossed the Sutlej and invaded British territory. Sir Hugh Gough, the British Commander-in-Chief, together with the Governor-General, hurried up to the frontier. Within three weeks four pitched battles were fought, at Mūdkī, Fīrozshahar, Aliwāl, and Sobrāon. The British loss on each occasion was heavy; but by the last victory the Sīkh were fairly driven into and across the Sutlej, and Lahore surrendered to the British. By the terms of peace then dictated, the infant son of Ranjīt, Dulīp Singh, was recognized as Rājā; the Jalandhar Doāb or tract between the Sutlej and the Biās was annexed; the Sīkh army was limited to a specified number; Major Henry Lawrence was appointed to be resident at Lahore; and a British force was detailed to garrison the Panjāb for a period of eight years. Sir H. Hardinge returned to England in 1848, and was succeeded by Lord Dalhousie [1].

He had not been six months in India before the second Sīkh war broke out. Two British officers were treacherously assassinated at Multān. Unfortunately, Henry Lawrence was at home on sick-leave. The British army was not ready to act in the hot weather, and despite the single-handed exertions of Lieutenant (afterwards Sir Herbert) Edwardes, the outbreak of fanaticism led to a general rising. The Khālsā army again came together, and once more fought on even terms with the British. On the fatal field of Chiliāṇwāla, which patriotism prefers to call a drawn battle, the British lost 2,400 officers and men, besides four guns and the colours of three regiments. Before reinforcements could come out from England, with Sir Charles Napier as Commander-in-Chief, Lord Gough had restored his own reputation by the crowning victory of Gūjarat, which absolutely destroyed the Sīkh army. Multān had previously fallen, and the Afghan horse (under Dost Muhammad) were chased back with ignominy to their native hills.

The Panjāb henceforth became a British province, supplying a virgin field for the administrative talents of Dalhousie and the two Lawrences. Rājā Dulīp

[1] *Imperial Gazetteer of India*, vol. vi. p. 411 ff.; or *Encyclopaedia Britannica* (ninth edition), vol. 20, pp. 111, 112.

Singh received an allowance of £58,000 a year, on which he retired as a country gentleman to Suffolk.

The first step in the pacification of the Panjāb was a general disarmament, which resulted in the delivery of no less than 120,000 weapons of various kinds. Then followed a settlement of the land tax, village by village, at an assessment below that to which it had been raised by the Sīkh exactions, and an introduction of a loose but equitable code of civil and criminal procedure. The system of roads and canals was greatly improved and extended by Colonel Robert Napier (afterwards Lord Napier of Magdala); and the security of British peace and the personal influence of British officers were felt to the furthest corners of the province. Thus it happened that, when the Mutiny broke out in 1857, the Panjāb remained not only quiet, but loyal, after only eight years' experience of British rule; while the North-West Provinces, which had been British territory for more than fifty years, rose in rebellion. The Sīkh population never wavered. Crowds of willing recruits came down from the Afghān hills. And thus the Panjāb, instead of being itself a source of danger, was able to furnish a portion of its own garrison for the siege of Delhi.

The Sacred Books of the Sīkh.

The Ādi Granth or 'first book' forms that part which is most generally revered. 'The Granth of the Tenth Reign' finds favour with the more fanatical section of the community. At present we have only an English translation of some part of the Ādi Granth, as translated by Professor Trumpp (1877).

The Ādi Granth is further subdivided as follows:—

1. The Jăpjī, which consists of introductory verses by Nānak, used after early bathing.

2. The Sō daru, consisting of extracts from Rāg Āsā and Rāg Gujrī, which is used by the Sīkh at evening prayer.

3. The Sō purkhū, or other extracts from Rāg Āsā.
4. The Sōhila, or three short sections, extracted from the Rāgs Gauṛī, Āsā, and Dhanāsarī, used as a prayer before retiring to rest.

The above pieces, being intended for devotional purposes, were therefore put at the beginning of the Granth.

5. The Rāgs, which form the body of the Granth, thirty-one in number, the first four being the most important [1].
6. The Bhōg, or conclusion of the Granth, containing thirteen portions, the last portion of which is always read in various ceremonies of the Sīkh.

In the above Rāgs the verses of different Gurū have been distributed, apparently without any leading principle, as hardly any verse is connected internally with another. It is to be noticed too that the name given to these portions implies the tune (Rāg) to which they are sung.

Turning next to *the language* of the Ādi Granth, it is easily inferred that 'the idiom is not the same throughout.' From a linguistic point of view the Granth is of great interest, because it forms a treasury of old dialects called *Gurmukhī*, specimens of which (in some cases) are nowhere else to be found. Gurmukhī, 'that which comes from the mouth of the Gurū,' is an antiquated form of Panjābi, which should be clearly distinguished from the modern Hindī of the North-West Provinces. The Granth contains sufficient materials to enable us to bridge the gap between the older Prākṛit dialects and the modern languages of the Aryan stock in India.

The sacred book is supposed to have been composed by at least thirty-five different authors, six of whom were Gurū, fourteen were Bhagat or saints, and fifteen were Bhaṭṭi or professional panegyrists. The dates of these authors must therefore be examined. Firstly, the Bhaṭṭi may be dismissed as probably

[1] e.g. Trumpp, *Ādi Granth*, pp. cxx, cxxi.

personal flatterers of Gurū Arjan, whose writings are quite valueless. Secondly, if Professor Trumpp is to be relied on, the oldest writer in the collection was *Namdev*, who lived about the fourteenth century. He is also considered the oldest Marāthi poet, and represents in his verses in the Granth some peculiarities of modern Marāthi. About the same time lived *Trilocan*, the Brāhman, who with Namdev was an inhabitant of the Deccan. *Jaidev* is also best placed as writing his Prākṛit verses during the fourteenth century, and not earlier, according to Lassen, or later, according to Wilson. Thirdly, the writings of Rāmānanda, Kabīr, and his fellow-disciples date back to the end of the fourteenth and the beginning of the fifteenth centuries, for they all write in old Hindī.

The only other writer in pure Hindī was Gurū Gōvind Singh, who lived two centuries later. For Nānak and his followers seem to have employed a mixture of two dialects, Panjābi and Hindī. There was a special reason for endeavouring to write in Hindī, for Hindī was the sacred language of all Indian devotees, and had been raised therefore to a kind of standard for religious compositions. It rapidly became unintelligible, however, to the people of the Panjāb.

It would be beyond our object to enter fully into the peculiarities of the idiom of the Granth. It is only necessary, therefore, to say here that the whole book is written in verse according to Hindū taste. It is noticeable that the measures of Sanskrit poetry have been discarded, and the metres are either Prākṛit metres or later inventions. The verses must rhyme together, but are only measured by quantity of space or pauses.

Cardinal Doctrines.

From what has been said above we shall expect to find in the religion of the Sīkh, not so much anything new, as an emphasis laid upon several ideas already familiar to the Hindū mind. The reforming element consisted just in this very reassertion of truth that had become hidden, and overgrown by superstition and religious observance. At the same time, in the study of the sacred Granth it is important to distinguish between the teachings of Kabīr and Nānak. Kabīr was not a Sīkh Gurū, but only a religious teacher who exercised profound influence over them. His teaching is essentially pantheistic, whereas theirs is a bold attempt at monotheism. Hence it comes that there are apparent contradictions in the Sacred Book, for many of his pantheistic utterances are incorporated in the Granth; and not only so, but they exercised influence over the phraseology of several succeeding *Gurū*, especially that of Arjan.

A. *The Unity of the Supreme Being is plainly asserted.* The very first line of the Adi Granth opens with the following attributes of the Deity :—One God (Ek-Uṇkār), the true Name (Sat-Nām), the Doer-Person (Karta-Purkh), without Fear (Nir-bhan), without Enmity (Nir-Vair), Endless Being (Akāl-murat), Uncreated (Ajūni-Seṇ-Bhiṇ). Compare also—

> 'Whom shall I call the second? There is none.
> In all is that one Spotless One. . . .'
> 'Know that there are two ways, but only one Lord.'
> 'There are six houses, six Gurū, six (methods of) instruction;
> The Gurū of the Gurū is One, the garbs many.'

The above three quotations come from Rāgs Gauṛī and Āsā, and are attributed to Nānak. They have evident reference to Brahmă, the Supreme Being; while the two ways and the six Gurū refer, on the one hand to Hindū and Mohammedan, on the other to various Hindū sects. But we must go deeper to find what relation the Supreme Being has to creation. Brahmă is only creator in the sense of being able to 'expand into plurality of forms.' For Arjan says:—'He himself is One and He himself is many[1].' Crea-

[1] Rāg Gauṛī, Mah. V., Sukhmanī XII. 6.

tures are led to consider themselves as individual beings, only because of *Māyā* (illusion), which the Absolute has spread out over the whole universe. All thereby fall into the errors of *egotism* and duality. The world is mere play and sport of the Absolute Being, which goes on expanding and contracting itself as it pleases. Brahmă, generally known as Hari, gives life and destroys *ad libitum*; e. g.—

> 'Between thee and me, me and thee, what is the difference?
> Like gold and the bracelet (made of it), like water and a wave[1].'

These words of Arjan are sheer Pantheism. A grosser and a finer kind of Pantheism does, however, exist in the Granth. The grosser identifies all things with the Absolute, the finer distinguishes between the Absolute and the finite being. The latter, as we have seen above, frequently rises to Theism, and represents God as not only uncontaminated by Māyā, but even distinct from His creation: e. g. 'Whose body the universe is, he is not in it, the creator is not in it.' In this finer shade of Pantheism creation assumes the form of *emanation from the Supreme*, as with the Sūfī. For either atomic matter is considered as co-eternal with the Absolute and immanent in It, or the reality of matter is more or less denied (and called τὸ μὴ ὄν), so that the divine is the only real essence in all. This last view borders on Idealism.

There are some differences in the teaching of Kabīr and Nānak with respect to idolatry. Kabīr ridicules it altogether as follows:—

> 'A stone is made the Lord, the whole world worships it:
> Who remains in alliance to this, is drowned in the black stream[2].'

But Nānak does not seem really to have forbidden the worship of other gods on the ground of the unity of the Supreme. Like many other Hindū teachers, he was contented with contending for the supremacy of Brahm.

[1] Sirī Rāg, Ravidās I.
[2] Rāg Gauṛī Purbī. of Kabīr, LII. 2.

B. *The Relation of Man to the Supreme.* The human soul is, as it were, 'scintilla animae divinae,' and so by itself immortal. It is the aim and object of the individual soul to be reunited with the fountain of light, from which it has emanated. No reason is given in the Granth for this emanation, but the return is cut off by works done in the body and by its impurity, of which second love or duality is the cause. These evils subject the soul to metempsychosis.

C. *The Origin of Sin.* Nānak did not deny that the world was under the dominion of sin. The object of his mission was to show mankind the way of escape from misery, and his means of escape will be considered later on. He fell into the common pantheistic conception of the Absolute being responsible for sin. The Granth plainly teaches that all creatures are subject to an absolute destiny. There are also passages which pointedly deny the 'Liberum arbitrium' in man. Even the gods are not excepted from Māyā. This is now and then keenly felt and acknowledged. Ravidās boldly asks—

> 'If I would not commit sins, O Endless One!
> How would thy name be "purifier of sinners"?'

Man then is impelled by three qualities (goodness, passion, and darkness). Under these influences and that of Māyā, he commits acts which subject the soul to transmigration.

D. *The Means of obtaining Emancipation.* The repetition of the name of Hari is the means whereby to drive away all the filth of sins, to liberate from all further transmigrations, and to unite with Hari. Whosoever mutters 'the name Hari' is saved in a moment. This would indeed have been too easy a way of salvation, had not the Sīkh Gurū safeguarded it. The name of Hari can therefore only be obtained from *the true Gurū,* who alone can bestow the rite of initiation and communicate the mantra of the name of Hari: e.g. 'By the true instruction of the *Gurū* he easily utters Hari.' In connexion with this initiation the doctrine of election is taught: e.g. 'Whose destiny it is, him the true *Gurū* unites (with Hari)[1].' But in order to prevent people from fatalism, inquirers are encouraged to seek the Lord, as follows:—

> 'Many are seeking the Lord.
> They obtain in their own heart the supreme Brahm[2].'

E. *Life after Death.* In no doctrine is the influence of Kabīr more widely felt than in the teaching of the Granth upon Nirvāṇa (Panjābi, Nirbāṇ). The immortality of the soul is asserted only so far as the idea of transmigration requires it. But when the soul has reached its highest object, it is no more mentioned.

Kabīr thus describes the process of reabsorption of the soul in the fountain of light[3]:—

> 'A drop is mixed with a drop.
> A drop cannot be separated from a drop.'

And again[4]:—

> 'When I was, thou (wast) not. Now art thou, and I am not.
> Now I and thou have become One, my mind is assured seeing One.'

This is exactly the pessimistic hope of the Buddha emerging again in the popular teachings of Indian mediaeval reformers, after having been expelled from India with Buddhism long before. The only difference consists in the means to obtain the desired end.

[1] Rāg Gauṛī, Mah. V., Sukhmanī V. 5.
[2] Ibid., Sukhmanī X. 6.
[3] Ibid., Kabīr, 29.
[4] Ibid., Kabīr, XXI. 1.

The Authority of the Gurū.

From the above standards of doctrine, we see that 'the *Gurū* is set up as the only infallible guide to complete emancipation.' He is the mediator between Hari and mankind; he is the boat that carries men over the water of existence; he is the very fullness of Hari himself. The disciple has therefore to submit to the direction of the *Gurū* unconditionally, mind and body, while the *Gurū* freely disposes of the treasures of Hari. It is fortunate that, according to the Granth, the *Gurū* need not exact much from his disciples to effect their emancipation. He gives him the name of Hari, enjoining him to mutter it continually. He requires him to repeat and sing the qualities of Hari, meditating upon them continually. He teaches him how to clear away his own 'ego,' and to consider himself as identical with the Brahm, pointing to this as the highest knowledge attainable. But in point of fact the *Gurū* has only one pantheistic sentence to teach:—'So ham,' i.e. 'I am that, I am identical with the Supreme.' And the three steps towards the attainment of this end are thus described:—

> 'First, by the One his own self was produced,
> Second, duality[1], and third, the threefold Māyā.
> The fourth step is the high step of the disciple,
> In which he is acquiring the perfectly True One[2].'

When this fourth step is obtained emancipation becomes complete. The soul need perform no religious works. Man has become totally *hopeless* in the world, and if he dies thus merged in meditation upon Hari, he becomes emancipated while in the body, and at death does not come again. Nānak says:—'The disciple remains absorbed' (in the Supreme)[3], i.e. in communion and fellowship.

[1] By duality is meant 'God, the subject, by creation becoming object.'
[2] Rāg Māgh, Mah. III, Asṭpad VI. 4.
[3] Rāg Gauṛī, Mah. III, Asṭpad I. 8.

Other Sīkh Observances.

Besides blind obedience to the *Gurū* there are a few other duties which each disciple must observe. The first consists of 'Service to the Saints,' which is considered as quite essential to salvation. Hence disciples are enjoined to wash the feet of the pious and to drink the water used in so doing; they should become a life-sacrifice to the holy men (sad-saṇgat), and should seek their society as the greatest blessing. Then come the triad of duties, namely, 'remembering the Name, giving alms, and practising ablutions.' The two latter are no longer duties, however, when the knowledge of Brahm has been obtained.

Occasional exhortations are given to abstain from falsehood, slander, and looking upon another's wife, besides purifying the heart from the five vices of lust, wrath, greediness, infatuation, and egotism. Charity to animal life, and therefore abstinence from animal food, was enjoined in early times. But the latter became a dead letter when the Sīkh became a military nation in the days of the tenth Gurū. Prayer to the Supreme is only recommended through the medium of the *Gurū*. On the other hand, Nānak is to be commended for recognizing, in advance of many teachers of his day, that secular business need form no obstacle to a religious life. He advised his followers to keep to their own occupations and not to leave the world.

To sum up the teaching of the sacred Granth of the Sīkh in a few words—we find salvation is said to depend upon the inward state of the mind, and not on outward things, and the social system of caste is not directly assailed by Nānak or his followers, until legally abolished by Gurū Gōvind Singh among the Khālsā body. So that though the teaching of the Veda and Purāṇa is reproved, the Brāhman is allowed to remain the family priest.

The Golden Temple at Amriṭsar[1].

In the present day much of the religious devotion of the Sīkh centres round the sacred Granth itself, and the shrine in which it rests, the 'Golden Temple' of Amriṭsar. This temple, called 'Har-mandar'—the temple of Hari—(or sometimes 'Durbār Sāhib), is one of the most striking sights in India. One must picture to oneself a large square sheet of water, bordered by a marble pavement. In the centre of the water rises the beautiful temple with its gilded dome and cupolas, approached by a marble causeway. In structure and appearance it may be regarded as a kind of compromise between a Hindū temple and a Mohammedan mosque, reminding one of the attempted compromise between Hindūism and Islām which was once a favourite idea both with Kabīr and Nānak. In point of mere size the shrine is not imposing, but the proportions seem nearly perfect. All the lower part is of marble inlaid with precious stones, and here and there overlaid with gold and silver. The principal entrance looks towards the north. The interior is even more gorgeous than the exterior. On the ground floor is a well-proportioned vaulted hall. Four short passages lead to this vaulted chamber. All around on the outside is a narrow corridor. In the interior, opposite the principal entrance, sits the Granthi scribe with the open Granth before him. He is attended by other officials of the temple, who assist him in chanting the sacred text. The Granth is indeed the real divinity of the shrine, and is treated as if it had a veritable personal existence. Every morning it is dressed out in costly brocade and reverently placed on a low throne under a jewelled canopy. All day long chowries are waved over the sacred volume, and every evening it is transported to the second temple (Akāl-Bungā), on the edge of the lake opposite the causeway, where it is

[1] Monier-Williams, *Religious Life and Thought in India*, p. 175 ff.

made to repose for the night in a golden bed within a consecrated chamber, railed off and protected from all profane intrusion by bolts and bars.

Population. Denominations.

The total population of Sīkh (that bear the name of 'Singh') in India, according to the Religious Census of 1891, numbers 1,907,833. Of these all but 37,000 live in the Panjāb, where they now form 7½ per cent. of the population. Their stronghold is the country between the rivers Ravī and Sutlej, including the historical cities of Lahore, Amriṭsar, Ambāla, and Jalandhar. In no district, however, do they form as much as 20 per cent. of the population.

From a religious point of view the followers of Nānak, exclusive of those who are the real Sīkh, form four leading denominations:

I. The Udāsī are a society of monks that reject the Granth of Gōvind Singh, and accept only the Ādi Granth. They have their own Gurū, who assumes spiritual authority. Their devotional service is simple, consisting of morning and evening song of praise, and playing upon the rebeck or violin. They have deviated from asceticism and taken up secular occupations. These Udāsī were founded by Sri Chand, the eldest son of Nānak, but are not recognized by the Sīkh.

II. The Suthrē (meaning 'pure') took their origin from Gurū Har-Raī. They are, however, renowned for their debauchery and drunkenness, and are to be found in every town in the Panjāb. They are a public nuisance, and are disavowed by the Sīkh, being mostly joined by profligates and vagabonds.

III. The Nirmatē Sādhū (pure saints) were originally strict Sīkh, and followed exclusively the Granth and Gōvind Singh. But then they became tinged with the Hindūism of the Shāstra and the Vēdānta, and so adopted the reddish-yellow instead of white robes. Now they mostly live in separate societies under a Gurū, and live a celibate life. Their brotherhood owns no caste, and they are largely established at Amritsar, being noted for their purity of morals.

IV. The Divānē Sādh (mad saints) keep their hair uncut like the Sīkh, and wear a necklace of shells, and a very large feather in their turban. They mostly consist of Jāts and tanners, and their devotional service consists only of muttering the true Name (of Hari).

But the most interesting body, from whom alone the real Sīkh of the present day come, are the Akālī (worshippers of the Timeless Being), who are said to have been instituted by Gōvind Singh. They were the zealots who firmly withstood innovations, and formed a powerful and dangerous body at the time of Sīkh independence, but are now dwindling away. They could be distinguished by their blue clothes. In those days also they directed the councils of the Gurmatā (or national council) in its deliberations, besides acting as defenders of the faith and presiders at religious ceremonies.

Christian Missions to the Panjāb.

For many years after the Indian Mutiny little fruit was seen among the Sīkh from the labours of Christian missionaries, though greater success was gained among Mohammedans. But the influence of missionary education has begun to tell, and recently a movement has been set on foot by several friends of the Sīkh, called the 'Khālsā Prayer Union[1].' It has taken for its motto, 'the Evangelization of the Sīkh in this generation,' and is rapidly interesting English Christians in the spiritual welfare of the Sīkh. The originator of the scheme, himself a Sīkh convert to Christianity, now studying medicine in England, belongs to the family of the Sīkh Gurū, and will give further information about the people that lie so near to his heart to any who care to make inquiries[2].

[1] Khālsā Prayer Union, *In His Name*, 1897, third edition.
[2] Address, Bābā Makhan Singh Soḍhī, London Hospital, E.

AUTHORITIES

Barth, *The Religions of India*, 40, 49, 72, 73, 77.
Bühler, *Sacred Laws of the Āryas*, 47.

Darmesteter, *Essay on the Mythology of the Avesta*, 14.
De Harlez, *Avesta*, 25.
Dosabhai Sorabji Karaka, *History of the Parsis*, 33, 36.

Elphinstone, *History of India*, 77.
Encyclopaedia Britannica, 79.

Fergusson and Burgess, *Cave Temples of India*, 66.
Fergusson, *History of Architecture*, 67, 68.

Haug, *The Five Gāthas*, 13.
Haug, *The Book of Ardā-Virāf*, 13.
Haug, *Essays on the Sacred Language, Writings, and Religion of the Parsis*, 15, 16, 18, 22.
Hunter, *Indian Empire*, 74.

Imperial Gazetteer of India, 79.
Indian Antiquary, 61.
In His Name, 91.

Lassen, *Indische Alterthumskunde*, 40, 45.

Monier-Williams, *Religious Life and Thought in India*, 69, 70, 71, 89.

Oldenberg, *Buddha, his Life, his Doctrine, his Order*, 40.

Pali Text Society, *Sumaṅgala Vilāsinī*, 62.

Rhys-Davids, *Buddhism, its History and Literature*, 48.

Sacred Books of the East, iv, 21, 22, 23, 24, 26, 32; v, xviii, xxiv, xxxvii, 13; xxii, 42, 43, 44, 48, 50; xxxi, 14; xlv, 44, 57, 58, 59, 60, 61.
Spiegel, *Age of the Avesta and Zoroaster*, 26.

Tawney, *Kathākoça*, 66.
Trumpp, *Ādi Granth*, 81.

Vienna Oriental Journal, 51.

Weber, *Indische Studien*, 40, 56.
Weber, *Sacred Literature of the Jains*, 49, 53.
West, *The Book of the Mainyō-ī-khard*, 13.
West, *Pahlavi Texts*, 13, 14, 15, 16.
Wilson, *Parsi Religion*, 21.
Wilson, *Essays and Lectures on the Religion of the Hindus*, 40.

INDEX